Talent

Talent

How new approaches to business
Values, Leadership & Organization
create a culture that attracts
The Best Talent

WALTER HALL

Auctoris Press

Auctoris Press
Norwell, MA

Published by

Auctoris Press

Auctoris Press
P.O. Box 274
Norwell, MA 02061
www.auctorispresspub.com
www.talentsolution.net

Talent by Walter Hall

ISBN-13: 978-0-9778023-4-0

LCCN: 2009912974

Publisher's Cataloging-In-Publication Data
(Prepared by The Donohue Group, Inc.)

Hall, Walter R.
    Talent / Walter Hall.

        p. : ill. ; cm.

    "How new concepts of business values, leadership and organization will help you
recruit and retain the best talent and dominate your market."
    Includes bibliographical references and index.
    1. New business enterprises--Management. 2. Corporate profits. 3. Success in business.
I. Title.

HD62.5 .H35 2007
658.11   2006933524

Book interior design by Peri Poloni-Gabriel
KnockoutDesign, www.knockoutbooks.com

Printed in the United States of America

Contents

Introduction

If all the management principles and concepts applied to the businesses I developed, the one key assumption that defined our core values, culture, policies, benefits, and everything else was this: with the advent and ever-increasing impact of a world economy that is technology- and information-based (requiring "knowledge workers") it became clear to me that the only sustainable competitive advantage left to any organization in the future was the quality of the human talent it could recruit, develop and retain – and the knowledge this talent brought with them and contributed to the organization while there.

Put another way, I saw our primary corporate assets as people and knowledge, guided by a set of ethical, practical values, maximized by enlightened leadership, and supported by an effective organizational structure. The majority of this book is devoted to the things we did to create and grow this asset.

THE KNOWLEDGE WORKER

We found the ideal employee to be self-directed, open-minded, professional, a team player, reliable, career-minded, flexible, and adaptive to constant change. We knew these were the key attributes required for someone to be comfortable and productive in our culture. This book describes how we successfully attracted and retained employees with these attributes.

CONTEMPORARY PRESSURES

We also found that these ideal employees shared some common contemporary pressures when trying to balance personal/family and business life, namely: dual income families, single head of household, child care, elder care, and economic uncertainty, to name the most prevalent challenges. This book describes how we developed values and policies that successfully relieved these pressures, making for a more productive, happy employee.

THE THREE PILLARS

All businesses strive for sustainable profit and growth. As mentioned above, all it takes is talent. For my companies, to attract and keep that talent it took the development and application of new concepts of business **Values, Leadership and Organization** (what we called "The Three Pillars" of Sustainable Profit & Growth) that created a culture that resonated with and attracted the best talent. This book is structured around *The Three Pillars* and describes and gives real-world examples of all three in action.

WALTER R. HALL, JR.

Norwell, Massachusetts

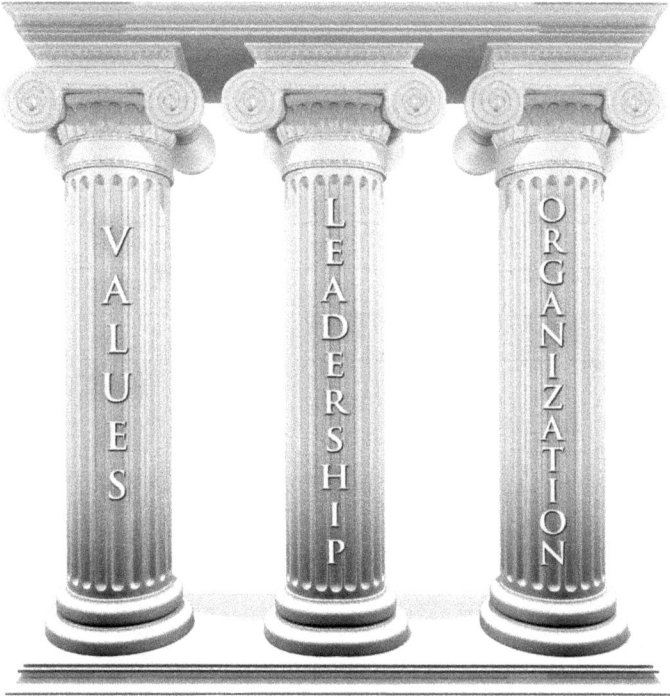

Fundamentals

BUILDING THE FOUNDATION

Part I of this book is designed to serve as a foundation for what follows. Here you'll find concepts and philosophies that apply or have relevance to all aspects of Values, Leadership, and Organization...The Three Pillars of Sustainable Profit and Growth.

My primary assumption is that readers of this book want to build or further expand a business enterprise that will develop a sustainable competitive advantage, resulting in consistent profit and growth over a long period of time. Other significant benefits include:

- ❖ The ability to recruit, develop, and retain the best human talent;
- ❖ The ability to provide a meaningful service;
- ❖ Long-term staying power; and
- ❖ Many enjoyment and personal-growth opportunities for many people.

This book is not about starting up a business enterprise. My assumption is that the readers have already addressed the essentials of doing just that: understanding the market, the needs of the customers, and the competition. Based on that knowledge, they've developed and are implementing an effective business plan describing *what* it is they're going to do, *why* they are going to do it, *how* they plan to do it, *when* they are going to do it, and *where* they are going to do it.

"SOMETHING VERY FUNDAMENTAL IS CHANGING"

"I've sensed for some time that something very fundamental is changing the way business has to be conducted in order to achieve sustained profit and growth in today's business world. I know there are many time-tested business principles that still apply—but now you have to balance these with new thinking that addresses the needs of today's unique work force. I couldn't put my finger on what that balance is really all about until I listened to you at the conference a few days ago."

This was a typical response to my presentation about our highly successful global company from executives of Fortune 500 and foreign companies, as well as numerous small business people around the world.

There really is a major paradigm shift taking place in the business world, and I believe *Talent* is one of the first to define it in all its many dimensions.

LONG-TERM PROFIT AND GROWTH

The major challenge facing all for-profit businesses is to achieve sustainable, long-term profit and growth, the primary evidence of life. The key word is *sustainable*. This is the toughest challenge facing every business.

When I first became involved in selling services to companies that in turn sold services at the retail level, it struck me that what they all were really looking for was what I ended up calling "the magic pill." Swallow it (painlessly) and you will miraculously become the dominant force in your market, possessing something special of high customer value that none of your competitors have. The only trouble is that there never has been any such magic pill. There is no easy, painless way to success, neither for individuals nor companies.

What many business people thought came close to the magic pill was the business *fad du jour* that periodically gripped the business community during the latter half of the twentieth century. These included fads like MBO (managing by objectives), conglomeration, re-engineering (shorthand for major staff reductions), CPI (continuous process improvement), Six Sigma, quality circles, T-groups, and the granddaddy of them all, the Internet, which many believed changed everything. A typical reaction to this particular fad went something like this: "So let's get the technology, and we'll crush the competition. You ask how we're going to apply it? We haven't figured it out yet—but we're afraid all our competitors are going to find out before we do."

Some of these fads were effective and live on, such as Six Sigma and the truly important idea of *quality*, which is now viewed as a profitable necessity, not an expensive add-on.

Conversely, many of the fads were disasters, like conglomeration, i.e., buying lots of disparate businesses with the theory that when one was down, another would be up. Most conglomerates that took shape in the sixties died in the seventies.

I cite this brief history of fads to point out that they all have one thing in common: the impact of talent or the lack thereof. That's the constant. It never changes. What has changed, however, is that there are now four other must-haves to compete successfully in the markets of the twenty-first century. The *best* talent now must also have the *best* knowledge, supported by the *best* values, leadership, and organizational structure. That's what's required to achieve that long-sought-after, elusive ideal of sustained profit and growth resulting from a sustainable competitive advantage. That's the real magic pill.

THE BEST PEOPLE

The term *best people* is of course relative and a bit of a misnomer (as is the so-called "best" of everything else). Every organization likes to brag that it has the best people, but as we all know, that is unachievable across the board. Once an organization grows beyond a few people, the immutable law of the bell-shaped probability (or *normal distribution*) curve comes into play. The vast majority of the employees will perform competently and similarly in the middle range of the bell, a few will perform exceptionally at the far right, and a few will perform poorly at the far left. This applies even in a top-flight organization with outstanding leadership, values, culture, and recruiting and selection processes. In that case, its bell-shaped curve will just be at an overall higher level than its competitors. In other words, it's all relative.

Be that as it may, I believe the best an organization can achieve in the best people category is to strive consistently to get uncommon results from common people. This is doable with enlightened leadership applying an ethical, practical set of fundamental beliefs that provide an environment and atmosphere that will do just that, i.e., result in uncommon results.

The bulk of this book is devoted to describing how developing and implementing an ethical, practical set of fundamental beliefs can create an organization that does, in fact, have the best people achieving uncommon results.

THE ELUSIVE MAGIC PILL

With the advent of information technology and the global economy, there are no longer any long-standing monopolies (sustained competitive advantages) like AT&T, the railroads, and the government-regulated airline industry.

Even though Microsoft, as I write, has what amounts to a desktop (and major applications) monopoly, you can start to see that the Web will be the platform of the future, where Google reigns supreme and Microsoft is an also-ran.

Microsoft appears to have the "big three"—Values, Leadership, and Organization—to maintain its growth and success, but perhaps not at its previous rate. It remains to be seen if Google has what it takes in the big three department to maximize its present advantage and potential.

As for many of America's premier growth companies that are now languishing, there is no doubt in my mind that most, if not all, have been lacking in one or more of the big three.

Take Coke, for example. The market for soft drinks had been declining for some time, but Coke didn't come up with any alternatives: most likely, this was a case of lack of leadership. Mattel had the same problem with its reliance on Barbie. Little girls don't play with dolls much any more.

Merck took a huge hit in September of 2004 when it had to withdraw Vioxx, one of its premier drugs, from the market. If Merck has strong and enduring Values, Leadership, and Organization it will come back. If it's lacking in even one of these contemporary success requirements, it will not.

One can say the same thing about Blockbuster, the onetime king of the video world, which has been hammered by video-on-demand and cheap subscription services.

These companies and their challenges and problems are just a few examples of life in the business world of the twenty-first century. I believe the only way to achieve success in the future is by recruiting, developing, and retaining high-quality human talent, reaping the benefits of the knowledge these employees bring with them and contribute to the organization while there. The absolute requirements to achieve this worthwhile objective are strong, enduring Values, Leadership, and Organization - what I call "The Three Pillars of Sustainable Profit & Growth."

ABOUT BUSINESS PLANS

There's an almost unlimited supply of books and articles about business plans by authors far more knowledgeable on the subject than I, so I'll just briefly comment on certain aspects of plans that have worked well for me or that I might have a slightly different wrinkle on.

The *What*

In the *what* category, I've learned to focus on and stress the primary value proposition the service or product will deliver and what makes it different and better than the competition. However, as Michael Treacy said in his book *The Discipline of Market Leaders*, "No company can succeed today by trying to be all things to all people. Choosing one discipline to master does not mean that a company abandons other important disciplines, only that it picks a dimension of value on which to stake its market reputation. The choice of one predominant value discipline, in effect, defines what a company does and, therefore, what it is."

Treacy felt there were three distinct value disciplines: operational excellence (low price and hassle-free service); product leadership (best product, period); and customer intimacy (best total solution for each customer's unique needs).

In building three major businesses from scratch, I came to strongly believe in this one-discipline approach. In my first business—local real estate—having no prior experience and being very young, I repeatedly stumbled trying to sell everybody everything everywhere all the time. I gradually and painfully learned to develop one product (full residential service) and concentrate on one specific segment of the market (single family homes in a certain geographic area).

In my second and third businesses, we really refined the concentration approach. In both businesses we had a nicely packaged bundle of services. At The Hall Institute, we positioned ourselves with our real estate firm clients as the *best total solution* for achieving their real estate sales objectives through education and training. In my third (global) business, our single market discipline/reputation was "The best total solution to our corporate clients' global employee relocation needs."

It's worth pointing out that the consultative sales approach is the only way to become successful under the best total solution discipline. In other words, how could we recommend certain services (from our bundle of services) unless we knew the client's specific needs? To determine those needs, we approached the prospective client in a consultative mode, which means the people we employed to sell the services had to have the knowledge and expertise to also perform them if called upon to do so.

The *Why*

In the *why* category, management must address the market for its products or services, i.e., what's the market's size, where is it located, what are the trends, who's the competition and, above all, what are the needs of that market?

Every time I think of market needs, I always think of Henry Ford, who said something like this: "If I could build a car that would sell for $500, I'd sell millions of them." The need? Automobile ownership at a reasonable price. Ford was right, and he found a way to meet his goal by using the production line. Need became opportunity became challenge became solution became success.

Over the years I was asked many, many times what I felt was the single most important reason for the success of the companies I was running. My answer was immediate and always the same: I attributed my success primarily to what I called *outside-in thinking*; that is, spending the majority of my time in the field, talking to clients and prospective clients and asking them what they felt they really needed—and really listening to their responses. No matter what the response, you could take it to the bank. Need becomes opportunity and then you must have the organization (the "in") to exploit that opportunity by developing a product or service that will meet (and exceed) that need better than anyone else. The key, of course, is to first listen and then correctly define the need. *Outside* is always first; *in* is the response.

The *How*

The *how* section of the business plan is the most voluminous; how tos always are. Usually, there are two major components to the how to section—the marketing plan and the financial plan.

It has been said that marketing takes a day to learn but a lifetime to master. So true. How does management plan to sell its product or service and what results does it expect? Most business plans that I've reviewed usually fail to address the real difference between marketing and sales (or selling).

The best definition I ever came across was penned by Ted Levitt in his book *Innovation in Marketing*. He said, "Selling concerns itself with the tricks and techniques of getting people to exchange their cash for your product. It is not concerned with the values that the exchange is all about. And it does not, as marketing invariably does, view the entire business process as consisting of a tightly integrated effort to discover, create, arouse and satisfy customer needs."

The last thought I'd like to share with you regarding the business plan is a subset of the marketing plan, the marketing strategy. In his great book

The Mind of the Strategist, Kenichi Ohmae defines *strategy* as "creating sustaining values for the customers far better than those of competitors." He goes on to say,

> Strategy starts with an ability to think in new and unconventional ways. One should avoid doing the same thing on the same battleground as the competition. The (primary) method of doing so is focusing on the key factors for success (KFSs). The most effective shortcut to major success seems to be to jump quickly to the top of the rank by concentrating major resources early on a single strategically significant function. *All of today's industry leaders, without exception, began by bold deployment of strategies based on KFS.* [emphasis mine]

I agree with Treacy and Ohmae. Concentration is the key to all economic results, which obviously assumes you've chosen the right thing to concentrate on. My father had a great way of illustrating this principle. He'd ask you to hold out your hand because he was going to throw you a single coin that he wanted you to catch, which you invariably did. Then he'd take a fistful of coins and ask you to catch them all with the same hand. Guess what happened.

ENTREPRENEURSHIP

I'm addressing this subject because it has relevance to the concepts and theories discussed in the balance of this book. If you are starting a new business enterprise—or looking to hire someone to do so—I hope my observations will be helpful regarding this aspect of starting a new business enterprise and keeping it growing, which is equally important.

I think most people have different ideas of what an entrepreneur is, so let me join the discussion. I took a quick look at my *American Heritage Dictionary,* which defines an *entrepreneur* as "A person who organizes, operates, and assumes the risk for a business venture." Not bad; I don't have any big disagreement. I like the "organizes" and "assumes the risk" part, but would question the relevance of "operate," which I will explain later.

To me, the essence of being an entrepreneur is, to use the parlance of poker players, to be willing at all times to go "all in" for the idea or enterprise you believe in. When I evolved my first business into a second business with virtually no capital available, I remortgaged our home three times in four years. Going from the second business to the third I did the same thing another three times, including second and third mortgages, some of them at outrageous rates. We can look back and laugh about it now, but those were some pretty tough and tenuous times for us. When this phase of our life was finally behind us, Judy jokingly told me that her right arm used to get sore from continually raising her hand and pledging that the execution of each of these mortgages was her "free act and deed." But she had faith in me. Every entrepreneur should be so fortunate.

Unless you can handle the pressure of an "all in" approach to building a business, being an entrepreneur is not for you. You must have total faith in yourself and your business venture and believe that no matter what happens, you can handle it. You get a good night's sleep every night. Over the years I've noted that this is the one personality dynamic that, if lacking, will stop would-be entrepreneurs dead in their tracks. If you can't stand the heat, stay out of the kitchen.

Know Thyself

I love to build and grow organizations. I view it as similar to creating a painting. Knowledge of the colors and tones and how you mix them are analogous, in my mind, to knowledge of marketing, sales, finance, information technology, human resources, training, and all the other functions that need to be combined to build and run a business—to create an organizational masterpiece. To me, there's nothing like it.

But please note that I said I "love to build and grow"—not "operate." If one loves the excitement, challenge, and creativity of building an organization, one doesn't necessarily enjoy the mundane, repetitive, boring tasks of running that organization on a day-to-day basis, with the need for memos, meetings, policies, procedures, and dealing with numerous personnel issues.

That's a pretty good description of me. However, in my last business I bit the bullet and stayed with the executive operating responsibility until the organization could afford to hire a competent president/COO and other top management.

I think it is at this point of growth that many entrepreneurs make a big mistake by hanging on and micromanaging the management team. In my experience you have to give the operating executives all the support in the world, but let them run with the ball. As founder, you must be willing, perhaps for the first time in your life, to acknowledge and listen to different and often opposing views of how to run the business. It is equally important that you be comfortable with letting them take *all* the credit for every success enjoyed by the organization.

This should pose no problem, provided you've hired the right talent. As chief entrepreneur and strategic planner in residence you need to mentally detach yourself from what you've built, think of your company as existing separately from you, and know that the ultimate success of what you've built will outlive you.

Many people can start a business. An effective entrepreneur can also keep a business growing.

PRODUCTIVITY

This subject has obviously been uppermost in the minds of the business world for quite some time, but in my opinion, the intensive focus on productivity dramatically increased during the nineties and continues to increase to this day.

The *American Heritage Dictionary* defines *productivity* as "producing abundantly; fertile; yielding favorable or useful results; constructive." Those are good definitions, but I'll simply settle for "the biggest bang for the buck"—or the ultimate dream of technology—"doing more with less." The phrase "peak efficiency" comes to mind as well.

In my third and last major company, Relocation Resources International (RRI), we were extremely labor intensive in our service delivery function. A typical client service team had an account manager (the client's primary contact), an account manager assistant, and six relocation counselors (the relocating employee's main contact), each of whom was assisted by a full-time relocation administrator. Total team count fourteen. We had a large number of teams in eight offices located in the United States, Canada, and the United Kingdom.

In the mid-nineties, we started to migrate from our old mainframe system to a wide area network throughout our entire organization, starting with our Global Service Group.

One of the biggest mistakes I ever made was incorrectly anticipating the impact of technology in this case. Going in, I felt that once our vastly expanded (and very expensive) new systems were fully installed, and everyone was trained, we could reduce the number of relocation administrators. That is, the new technology would greatly increase efficiency (productivity), so much that we would need only one relocation administrator for every two or three relocation counselors. This would result in cost savings in our service group in the millions of dollars range. More for less—wow!

So once the new system was fully operational, I really pushed the head of our Global Service Group to make that move and strive to assimilate as many of the excess relocation administrators as possible throughout the company.

She did, and the results were a disaster. Case loads skyrocketed, calls from clients and relocating employees were not returned in a timely manner (or not at all), billing was late because we weren't recording all the data needed for complete billing, and on and on.

We ultimately recovered without losing a single client. However, it was a close call, caused a lot of turmoil, and was a severe blow to the morale of our service group team, who also needed time to recover.

It didn't take me and service group management very long to figure out that the new system required much more input (and time to input) than the old mainframe system, and the real payback for the new technology was not fewer staff, but more info. The new system gave us a quantum leap in the amount of valuable data that was of inestimable value to our corporate clients and our management staff in the form of meaningful, real-time analysis of such things as client and transferee (relocating employee) response time, forecasting of case loads, and so much more. There was a great benefit for the cost, but it turned out to be quite different than I had originally anticipated.

As additional reinforcement, just as the light was dawning that the real payback was *more info*, I read an article in the December 3, 1993 *Wall Street Journal* titled "Be Data-Literate—Know What to Know," by management guru Peter F. Drucker. In this article he said:

> Executives have become computer-literate. But not many executives are information-literate. They know how to get data. But most still have to learn how to use data. Few executives yet know how to ask: What information do I need to do my job? When do I need it? In what form? And from whom should I be getting it? Fewer still ask: What new tasks can I tackle now that I get all these data? Which old tasks should I abandon? Which tasks should I do differently? Practically no one asks: What information do I owe? To whom? When? In what form?

We used these key questions as our road map to quickly maximize our newly acquired goldmine of information.

Looking back, the lesson we learned was this: lacking experience in evaluating and projecting the impact of new technology and major systems conversions, we should have sought out the expertise of other companies that had already gone through the process and asked a simple question: "What did you expect and what did you actually get?"

The Ultimate Productivity Synergy

The application of, and the benefits to be derived from, technology are greatly enhanced when adopted by the type of organization described in this book: one dedicated to developing a long-term, sustainable competitive advantage based on the quality of the human talent it can recruit, develop, and retain, and the knowledge employees bring with them and continue to develop and expand upon while with the organization.

The extent of productivity in the application of all the tools available in all facets of the business enterprise rests solely with the quality of the organization's human talent and knowledge, supported by enlightened leadership. As always, people, knowledge, and leadership are the keys to success.

THE "S" GROWTH CURVE

Consider the classic four-phase business growth curve: extended build-up, "lift-off," prolonged rapid expansion, and, ultimately, leveling off, or maturity, at the top of the curve.

However, as happens in so many cases, over time the S curve turns into the bell shaped curve of life, i.e. the ultimate downhill curve, eventually tapering off into nothingness (the death of a business).

Case studies of corporate deaths—including, for example, such giants as Montgomery Ward, Polaroid, DEC (Digital Equipment Corp), and

Enron—clearly indicate that the primary cause of corporate deaths is ineffective, incompetent, and/or larcenous top management and, by implication, similarly ineffective company directors.

In most cases, what exacerbates this type of a top management situation is lack of any meaningful, ethical, professional core values imbedded in the corporate culture over an extended period of time. There will be much more on this subject later in the book.

I believe that if the fourth business phase, maturity, is just maintained on a "housekeeping" basis, without any attempts at regeneration, it will, in fact, atrophy and evolve into the bell shape and ultimate death.

The ideal, over an extended period of time, is to keep building new S curves that start off with a new phase one, i.e., build-up, that replaces the phase four/maturity of the preceding S curve. This, in essence, is what I did with three businesses; one evolved into the other. Each new S curve required fresh thinking and total regeneration from top to bottom throughout the organization. And the outstanding, flexible staff from each preceding company segued nicely into each new company.

However, this regeneration approach doesn't only work for businesses evolving into new businesses. The approach can apply to the same company regenerating itself based on new realities, too; for example, in response to new opportunities to achieve sustained profit and growth or, on the other extreme, the decline of a market that places companies serving that market in a survival mode.

THE SERVICE INDUSTRY

I've spent my entire adult life involved in three businesses within the service industry, with no durable goods to manufacture, no inventory to maintain, and no product distribution network—just people with knowledge, ideas, business acumen, and many fiduciary relationships.

However, having spent considerable time with high-level management in many major manufacturing companies (Boeing, Pfizer, 3M, and Proctor & Gamble, to name a few), I came to the realization that the concepts and principles that served my companies well are applicable to companies of all sizes, in all industries. We all are primarily dependent on people with knowledge, supported by effective leadership.

It's a pretty accepted management principle today that keeping existing customers is far more cost-effective than getting new customers. Or, perhaps better said, you'll always realize a net loss replacing a lost customer with a new customer of approximately the same volume.

Having said that, consider this example: a steel company sells to a variety of heavy construction companies building commercial buildings, bridges, and the like. Their product and its cost to produce (absent raw material cost) is definitely a function of its people, their knowledge, and company leadership. If they're superior, the product will be high quality and the price competitive.

If this capability also applies to the marketing and sales effort, all should be well. But here's an example of what can happen in the real world: the construction company places an order with its sales rep, and it's not delivered in time. Repeated calls to the rep and the order-processing department fall on deaf ears, and when the construction company does finally speak to someone, it's obvious to the caller that they couldn't care less. In other words, service is lousy. The service attitude isn't there. The result? The steel company loses an established customer, which a major competitor picks up. This is a big loss for one, and a big gain for the other. Compounding the problem is the fact that when things like this occur in the service cycle, it impacts the sales effort of getting new customers and their dollars to replace the lost customers and their dollars. In other words, if service is lousy with existing customers, it usually equates to difficulty closing potential customers.

My point is that the same scenario could apply to a company in the service industry. That's why I believe the proven concepts and principles addressed in this book are applicable to business enterprises of all sizes, in all industries.

The ideal, of course, is for *every* employee of the company to deal with customers like an owner would. Even if it's unspoken, the feeling of pride and loyalty of being part of a great organization transmits itself through the phone, or e-mail, or on a face-to-face basis. It's evidenced by employees who answer the phone promptly instead of letting it go into voice mail, greet customers with a smile and make them feel important instead of ignoring them, and on and on and on.

Unrealistic, you say? Absolutely not. I had this kind of great customer service in spades in my business for the last twenty-five years. This book will explain exactly how this was accomplished.

SALES AND SERVICE

Until fairly recently in the annals of American business, sales and service were the "big two" functions, and many times marketing was viewed as synonymous with sales. All the other functions in the corporate world, i.e., finance, human resources, information technology, purchasing, administration, and others supported them.

Let me share with you my philosophy on sales and service. First, they're inseparably connected. If the sales staff makes the promise, "If you buy this product it will do this and that," then the service staff has to deliver on that promise. Therefore, if these two functions aren't interconnected, the service staff will always end up saying things like "We don't do that," while the customer will say "Your service stinks—this product is nowhere near what we thought we were buying."

You connect sales and service by considering sales and service staff, along with marketing staff and the rest of the corporate staff, to be all part of the same team, not allowing them to form vertical barriers between functions. Horizontal is the way to go. The motto should be, "We're all involved in the success of this company and we all contribute to that success."

For example, if the information technology staff doesn't produce timely, accurate, and meaningful reports, or the finance staff doesn't get accurate bills out on a timely basis, those are just two more negative impacts on the company's service in the eyes of the customer.

The best companies seat all functions of the company at the same table. It's all marketing/sales and service. It's all about PEOPLE.

CLIENTS AND CUSTOMERS

Throughout this book, you will find I use these words quite often. I have found over the years that many people use these two words interchangeably and therefore incorrectly.

A *client* is a person or entity that has contracted with a supplier to perform a service. The relationship is one of principal and agent, where the supplier is obligated to protect and promote the interests of the client as if the client were its own.

A *customer* is a person or company that receives goods and/or services from a supplier. The relationship is essentially of a fiduciary nature, i.e., one involving confidence and trust. Additionally, the customer (as well as the client in this case) is entitled to a standard of reasonable business care.

In all three of my businesses, we dealt with both clients and customers. In the real estate business, home sellers were always our clients because they paid our fees (commissions). The buyers of these homes we dealt with were our customers.

At The Hall Institute of Real Estate, we sold our agent and management training services to major real estate firms throughout the country. They were our clients. They paid our fees. All the agents and managers we trained were our customers.

In the global relocation business, the corporation we contracted with was our client and their relocating employees were our customers. To reinforce this, we viewed and conducted ourselves as if we were a department of the client company.

Part I Highlights
Points to Remember

The Best People

The *best people* are common people who give you uncommon results.

About Business Plans

Companies must understand and appreciate their primary value proposition. They have to define what makes them different and better than their competitors. They must understand and appreciate the true needs of their market and the difference between marketing and sales.

Entrepreneurship

Like the best poker players, true entrepreneurs are willing to go "all in."

Productivity

E-mail technology, coupled with greatly expanded information availability, has resulted in one of the greatest increases in productivity ever.

The "S" Growth Curve

To avoid the bell-shaped curve, constantly regenerate.

The Service Industry

Successful concepts of the service industry also apply to the manufacturing industry.

Sales and Service

All organizational functions ultimately fit into marketing/sales and service, so all functions should have a seat at the strategic planning table.

CLIENTS AND CUSTOMERS

If you're serving clients, you're obligated to protect and promote their interests as if they were your own. Customers involve a fiduciary relationship—one that requires confidence and trust.

PART II

Values

ELIMINATING CORPORATE MELTDOWNS

Had the founders, directors, and/or shareholders of Enron, World Com, MCI, and Tyco (to name just a few of the pillaged and mismanaged companies of the recent past) established practical, ethical core values for their companies early on and worked hard to deeply imbed them over time, it would have been much more difficult for the now-convicted leadership to build a house of cards and line its own pockets in the process, at the expense of employees, shareholders, and creditors.

With the concepts and philosophies described in Part I as a base, it's time to build the foundation upon which your business enterprise can be established or further developed—a foundation that will deliver consistent profit and growth, stand the test of time, produce a world-class product and/or service, and provide lots of enjoyment and personal growth opportunities for lots of people.

Let's assume you've finished your business plan and are getting ready to launch your new business enterprise. After taking a much-deserved break (twenty-four hours), you make the tough decision to block off three uninterrupted days to put pen to paper and describe all the fundamental beliefs upon which you want to build your organization. You know that when you actually start operations, you'll have precious little time to do anything but assemble all the resources you need to get started. So, if you want to document your fundamental beliefs, it's now or never.

In order to get yourself psyched up properly, you pull out of your management/leadership file a quote from Thomas Watson in his book *A Business and Its Beliefs*:

> Success or failure can be traced to the question of how well the organization brings out the great energies and talents of its people. What does it do to help these people find common cause with each other? And how can it sustain this common cause and sense of direction through the many changes which take place from one generation to another? The answer comes through a sound set of beliefs, on which it premises all its policies and actions. Next, I believe that the most important single factor of corporate success is faithful adherence to those beliefs…beliefs must always come before policies, practices and goals. The latter must always be altered if they are seen to violate fundamental beliefs.

Based on my experience in building three successful businesses over a forty-four–year period, I've obviously developed some very strong beliefs of my own. As the decade of the nineties unfolded I crystallized one particular view of the business world that would grow to impact all my fundamental beliefs from then on: with the increasing maturity of the global economy and information technology taking hold in the late twentieth century and growing in significance exponentially ever since, I came to believe that the only sustainable competitive advantage any business could achieve in the future would be the quality of the human talent it could recruit, develop, and retain, and the knowledge well-selected and loyal employees brought with them and continued to develop and expand upon while with the organization.

People—the best people—coupled with knowledge that continues to grow keeps the organization ahead of the competition.

Peter Drucker, in his book *The Age of Discontinuity*, put it this way: "The world is becoming not labor intensive, not material intensive, not energy intensive, but knowledge intensive." I believe it. In the twenty-first century, the demand for knowledge workers is projected to far exceed the supply.

At RRI, we documented our fundamental beliefs that supported this people/knowledge philosophy. I think it was Socrates who said, "Wisdom starts with a clear definition of words." Following are my definitions of the key subjects comprising the wisdom of fundamental beliefs that once again are grounded in the people/knowledge philosophy.

ON SERVICE

Permeating my fundamental beliefs is the concept of service. During the last half of the twentieth century, our economy in the United States evolved from primarily a manufacturing base to what has been referred to as a service economy. However, I think the word *service* is still grossly misunderstood or, at the least, misinterpreted by the very people who are supposedly responsible for providing it.

Several years ago, when our cable service was provided by AT&T, I went to the local office one day to inquire about a digital unit. I walked into the office and saw what looked like bank teller windows directly ahead with two women sitting on stools behind the glass partition openings. There were no customers there, so I walked right up to one of the windows. As I was walking towards them, I noted that the two service reps were holding quite an animated conversation, which continued when I came up to the window. No acknowledgement that I was there. No break in their conversation. I stood there waiting to be served for quite some time. When I ran out of patience, I raised my voice a few degrees and said "Hello in there—I'm your customer and I pay your salary and provide your benefits," whereupon the woman in front of me tore herself away from her fellow employee and swiveled her head in my direction with a disgusted "You've got to be kidding" expression on her face. A brief and heated discussion ensued, with the result that I left her as service-insensitive as I found her. Wouldn't you think a company in the service business would make absolutely sure that all its employees knew who paid their salary and provided their benefits? I believe AT&T isn't in the cable business today and, in fact, is less than half the company it used to be. Serves them right.

And how about the old king of the retailers, Sears, Roebuck and Co.? It only happened to me twice, but that was enough. I never went back. On both occasions, I picked out some tools and then had to walk around the store for a long time trying to find someone to take my money. No wonder they're now a second-rate outfit.

I'm sure you've had the same experience as I have when going out to dinner at a new restaurant. You can quickly tell if the owner is service oriented. Are you greeted immediately and cordially? Are they really happy to have you visit their establishment? When you sit down at your table, does your server let you know within the first few minutes that he/she is going to be the person to serve you and is happy to do so? Even if they have too many tables to serve, a brief "I'll be with you in a minute" works wonders.

And how about those municipalities that have a monopoly on providing services to their taxpaying citizens? On a positive note, with the advent of professional city and town managers, it's very interesting to experience for the first time a bit of real service by municipal employees. It appears they are beginning to realize that the taxpaying citizens in their municipality provide their salary and, in some cases, extensive benefits. Here in Massachusetts, we started experiencing for the first time a small degree of the same service orientation by state employees under the governorship of Mitt Romney. It is interesting to note that he had extensive experience in running a successful business before becoming governor.

With that background on my observations, herewith are my thoughts on the subject of service. Simply stated, I believe that *service satisfaction* keeps a company in the competitive ball game, win a few, lose a few, whereas *service delight* will not only consistently win the game but deliver the league championship and maybe even the World Series.

Service satisfaction occurs when customers get what they expect; no more, no less. This, of course, should lead to the correct conclusion that the key to service satisfaction is to clearly understand customers' expectations. In a competitive environment, most win a few, lose a few companies learn this by trial-and-error experience, when they try to find out why they're losing customers.

The champs, on the other hand, have carefully researched the matter (through surveys, for example) and make it a point to ask their customers how they felt about the service and then listen to the answer. They also reward their staff for exceeding service satisfaction (i.e., attaining service delight) on a consistent basis. They celebrate it company-wide on every possible occasion. As you can well appreciate, commitment to service delight is a big part of the champs' core values and culture.

Many frequent business travelers, including yours truly, have come to judge the quality of a hotel's service primarily through room service. In the old days, you'd call down the night before and ask for breakfast delivery at a specific time and the response usually was that they would strive to deliver as close to that time as possible. Then you'd keep your fingers crossed. Often the results were hit or miss. Sometimes service satisfaction, sometimes not.

Then someone, somewhere, dreamed up the breakfast request form you put on the door before 2:00 a.m., with time of delivery choices in thirty-minute increments. The hospitality industry quickly found out that thirty-minute increments did not meet customers' expectations and quickly reverted to fifteen- or twenty-minute intervals. If the customer requested breakfast to be delivered between 6:45 and 7:00, service satisfaction was attained if this occurred, perhaps with a five-minute leeway on either end. But service satisfaction will not make for a great company. Only consistent service delight will.

Service delight occurs when customers consistently get more than they expect. I'll give you an example: in a hotel I frequented in Denver, the very enterprising general manager came up with a system to ensure, in almost every case, exact-time room service delivery. You either called room service or left the form on the door the night before and specified the exact time you wanted your breakfast delivered. My initial expectation was to allow a few minutes either way. But guess what? Of the twenty-odd times I stayed there, only twice did they miss the exact time delivery (by just a few minutes) and on both occasions, I got a call from the concierge or general manager himself apologizing for the delay. It was so great to hear that knock on the door at the exact time requested. Did I love this place? You bet. Did I recommend it to others? Yes, many, many times. Were they usually booked? Always. Were they profitable? Obviously.

I should point out that as with all service-delight experiences like this one, the excellence of service was not an isolated event. It was just one more manifestation of a very service-oriented culture and core values. Housekeeping was responsive and attentive, as were the concierge, doormen, and front desk.

Service Recovery

No description of service is complete without at least a few comments on this subject.

During my early hours in the ROTC flight-training program, my instructor drummed into me that recovery was the single most important talent I could ever develop. His point was this: no matter how good a pilot you are, you are going to have problems, a few of which could be life-threatening. My first experience with this philosophy really hit home when, on my first solo flight as I was coming in for the landing, I stalled out at about fifteen feet above the runway. Had I not quickly recovered by jamming the throttle in and then leveling off again for a relatively smooth landing, the government would have had to spring for some big bucks to pay for the damaged landing gear and I would have had a big black mark on my record.

Over the years I've had a number of experiences, as I'm sure you have, where service recovery was definitely called for but not always delivered. Recently, my wife and I and another couple went to a restaurant where we had enjoyed the food and service on one previous occasion. However, on this night, the food was lousy and the service almost nonexistent. When the maitre d' was making the rounds, he stopped by our table and asked how we were enjoying the meal, whereupon I told him flatly that the food and service were terrible. His smile vanished, he froze a bit, babbled a few unintelligible words and walked away, ensuring that we would never come back again and encouraging us to tell other people about our bad experience.

Compare that to the same circumstances we experienced at another restaurant (poor food quality/marginal service), whereupon the owner immediately and profusely apologized, said the entire meal was on him, gave us a gift certificate to come back again, and followed that with free after-dinner drinks. Because of this approach, we were inclined to believe his story that the problem occurred when the chef went home sick and that it wouldn't happen again. In fact, we found that to be the case as we have frequented this restaurant many, many times since this occurred.

My point is that in a service business, service foul-ups are bound to happen. When they do, it's imperative that the whole organization view them not as a problem, but as an opportunity not only to recover, but to further cement the service relationship. The key is immediate recognition and acceptance that there is a legitimate problem (with a no-excuses approach) followed by immediate action.

In their book, *Satisfaction*, authors Chris Denove and James Power stressed that customers who run into problems—but whose problems are handled swiftly and politely—actually wind up being more loyal than customers who never encounter a problem in the first place. This certainly verified my own experience.

The bottom line is that failed businesses are no longer around because they didn't even achieve service satisfaction. Mediocre business enterprises merely survive through service satisfaction. Top organizations stay on top with service delight, because they clearly understand and are fully committed to consistently exceeding their customers' expectations. And they realize, in this competitive world of ours, that expectations invariably keep rising, so these top companies always find ways to constantly keep their fingers on their customers' ever-accelerating pulse.

ON SURVIVAL

My approach to recognizing and addressing the reasons for an organization's survival may be a bit unique, but I would nonetheless like to share this approach with you because it has served me exceptionally well over the years.

Essentially I found that the key to survival preparation is being aware, on an organizational basis, of the one thing that most accounts for the success *and* survival of the organization. At RRI, that was, simply, getting and keeping corporate clients.

We fervently believed that all employees must have it in their gut that their paychecks, benefits, job security, and growth opportunities rested solely with the collective ability of everyone in the organization to get and keep clients. As you read on, you'll note this principle reinforced in our mission, vision, core values, culture, and strategy. The necessity of getting and keeping clients was reinforced on a consistent basis in every possible communication venue inside the company and with our service partners as well. It was THE key performance measurement.

Sam Walton, founder of Wal-Mart, said this: "There is only one boss. The customer. And he can fire everybody in the company from the chairman on down simply by spending his money somewhere else." Wal-Mart's continuing success is directly related to this philosophy, which I know is deeply imbedded throughout the entire, huge, Wal-Mart organization. Keep that customer happy and coming back for more; otherwise he might spend his dollar somewhere else.

There is, however, another dimension to survival that relates to events over which the organization and its management have little or no control—for example, tragedies like 9/11, or paradigm shifts like DVDs replacing VHS, automobiles and airplanes steadily reducing the demand for railroads, etc. The market is, has always been, and will always continue to be dynamic.

Here's how we addressed external survival impacts at RRI. In an orientation video for new employees, I said:

> I've just explained how getting and keeping clients is our single most important company-wide objective, and one that you and all your fellow employees directly control. Our success *and* survival depend on it.

> However, there could be external events that could impact our company negatively over which we have little or no control that could affect everyone's job security, including mine. There could be major shifts in the way corporations relocate employees; there could be national tragedies and major economic recessions that could seriously impact our business.

You've already reviewed our RRI/Employee *Mutual Expectations*, but let me repeat one relevant statement of what all employees can expect from the company, and that is: honesty in advising about corporate objectives and the current and projected economic viability of the company.

What this means is that you can rest assured we will keep you fully advised of all the good and bad things that may be happening which could impact the company and therefore, potentially, your job. If we see some external problems occurring that we feel could negatively impact the company, you'll be the first to know, and we will also advise you as to what we're doing about it.

MISSION

Your mission statement is, essentially, the what, who, where, and why of your company. The RRI mission statement said: "We help our corporate clients relocate their employees around the world with the least inconvenience, stress, and loss of productivity, and we do it all at a reasonable cost."

This had all the elements of a good mission statement: it tells *what* we did, *who* our client was, *where* we operated (the world), and a meaningful *why*—minimizing stress and lost productivity. A December, 1994 article in *Fortune* magazine entitled "Why Do People Work" said, "Psychologists say that people who can create a rationale for their work usually get more out of it." I agree. At RRI we provided critical support services to over 15,000 of our corporate clients' employees (and their families) being relocated around the world every year. All RRI employees felt they were providing a meaningful service because they believed in our mission and its expanded internal description, a portion of which stated: "We help relocating employees and their families, during one of the most stressful times in their lives, settle into their new environment with the least stress and inconvenience." When one of these relocating employees, or his or her spouse, sent us a service critique that said "Thanks—we couldn't have done it without you," it was a cause for pride, celebration, and recognition.

VISION

My Dad used to say, "Unless you know where you're going, any path will take you there." Your vision statement is the *where*, as in "Where are we all going?" Here's the vision statement we developed at RRI in 1999, when RRI was ranked number five in a field of over twenty major competitors: "By 2005, we will be recognized within the global mobility community (companies that relocate employees, relocation professionals, service providers, and consultants) as the Number One Quality Relocation Service Company, as evidenced by client growth, retention, and service satisfaction."

This was, in essence, RRI's five year plan, or vision, in a nutshell. However, with every vision, one should always document, concurrently, the specific measurements that will be used to determine if, in fact, the vision is being or has ultimately been achieved. At RRI, we said:

We will know that we have achieved our vision when **all** of the following have been accomplished: our transferee volume clearly positions us as one of the top three relocation companies worldwide; our transferee service satisfaction level (as polled by independent sources) is the highest in the industry; we have retained our existing clients and have a significant pipeline of desirable clients wishing to partner with RRI; we have achieved manageable, annual new client growth without compromising the level of service to our existing clients; and we have a pipeline of highly qualified relocation professionals seeking employment with RRI.

It's important to point out that every employee in the company was involved in the development of this vision and, equally important, its measurement. It's true—people support what they help create.

Keeping the Vision Alive

It's all well and good to go through an extensive exercise to come up with a meaningful vision. However, as always, follow-through is equally important. Follow-through requires the continuing attention of top management, from the CEO on down. As an example, here's a reprint of a typical regularly scheduled "keep the vision alive" e-mail to all employees from me:

To: All RRI Employees
From: Walt
Date: December 11, 2000
Subject: Year 2000

I'd like to take this opportunity to extend my personal best wishes to you and yours for a wonderful holiday season and once again say a big 'THANKS' for helping RRI achieve success in a very challenging year.

As CEO, you know that one of my primary jobs is to look ahead, evaluating all those factors that could affect—either positively or negatively—the achievement of our **Vision 2005.**

I'm very pleased to tell you that we have made significant progress in achieving all the Vision 2005 "Specific Measurements" that we all established. We have already hit three of these criteria, are about halfway along with two, and are approximately 25 percent on one. So, I give it a 'weighted' 70 percent overall (last year we rated it at 60 percent).

Because of this and a more streamlined organization recommitted to basics, I have never been more confident that the forthcoming year will be the best in RRI's history. You're the best, and I'm proud to be associated with you.

—Walt

CORE VALUES

Core values are the philosophical convictions guiding the organization on a successful journey. I return to the description Tom Watson gave of core values: "A sound set of beliefs on which [a company] premises all its policies and actions—beliefs must always come before policies, practices and goals. The latter must always be altered if they are seen to violate fundamental beliefs." Here were RRI's core values:

> Through never-ending business cycles, RRI's traditions and values remain constant—based on a foundation of five strongly held beliefs.

Client Focused

Using RRI's *Performance Standards* as a guide, we strive continually to exceed our clients' expectations, which is the primary reason for our continued growth and success. We are committed to manageable growth that never compromises our service delivery to existing clients. The key to being client focused is to also be equally employee-centered.

Employee Centered

We recruit, develop, and retain self-directed, professional, careerminded people and provide them with a stimulating work environment, a comprehensive salary and benefits package (including employee stock ownership), and employee policies that address the contemporary challenges of balancing work and personal demands.

Leadership Driven

RRI is committed to providing strong leadership that can assure clients of consistent quality service and maintain RRI's growth so that employees have job security and further personal growth and career opportunities.

Performance Oriented

Our judgment of how well we are doing as a company, as teams, and individually is based on achieving challenging, clearly defined performance objectives.

The Power of Partnering

We are committed to building a long-lasting partnership with each of our clients. Partnering also means respecting our preferred service partners and their role as an integral part of the RRI service-delivery team.

Our core values certainly weren't developed overnight. In the early stages, most of our energies and resources were devoted to building a viable organization recognized as such within the industry. During this period, we had few employees and few clients.

At our peak in the early part of the current century, we had 375 employees, over 2000 domestic accredited representatives, 850 global accredited representatives in 110 countries, and seven offices in the United States, Canada, and England.

A great deal transpired during the ensuing years between the build-up and maturity phases of our S growth curve, which related mostly to the quantity and quality of both our staff and our clients.

I think most companies in their early build-up phase simply have neither the time nor the need to address and describe their core values and other fundamental beliefs in detail. However, most companies in their early stages do see the need to succinctly describe, for the outside world, who they are and what they do. It also serves as a good internal reality check as well.

We took our first serious pass at describing our core values in 1986 when we were just past our lift-off phase and beginning the prolonged rapid expansion phase, starting to aggregate a large employee and client base. In retrospect, what we came up with in 1986 held us in very good stead as a base for many years. Until the mid-nineties, we had relatively minor revisions to our core values. However, the actual RRI core values described above took their formative shape when our people and knowledge orientation jelled in the mid-nineties.

Starting in the mid-eighties, our core values were reviewed at least once a year by the management staff and every third year were opened up for review by the entire company. We asked for recommendations for additions, revisions, and deletions; in essence, we were updating to reflect current realities.

Thinking of core values makes me also think of the many corporate scandals of the late nineties and early part of the current century. I strongly believe that had the founders, directors, and/or senior management of Enron, World Com, MCI, and Tyco established morally based, ethical core values for their companies early on and worked hard to deeply imbed them in their organizational culture, it would have been, at the least, much more difficult for the leadership to build a house of cards and line its own pockets in the process at the expense of the employees, shareholders, and creditors.

The misdeeds of these and other individuals in positions of trust in the business world have hurt the image of the vast majority of business people who conduct their businesses with integrity and related business values. Public trust is quickly lost and slowly won back. Hopefully, as I write this book, we've started on the long, slow path back to the public trust that most businesses deserve.

Values and Profitability

There is a direct correlation between core values and profitability, and there are many examples that illustrate this relationship. I'll cite just one that's indicative of all those consistently profitable companies that have a long-term, fully imbedded, quality set of fundamental beliefs, including core values and culture. These two, collectively, are the key beliefs that relate to a company's relationships with its employees, customers, clients, and service suppliers.

The world's largest and most diversified health care company is Johnson & Johnson, which is also viewed by the investment community as one of the consistently best managed and most profitable companies in the world.

In 1943, the founder, General Robert Wood Johnson, wrote and first published the *Johnson & Johnson Credo*, a one-page document outlining J & J's responsibilities to customers, employees, the community, and stockholders. This was, in essence, its core values. Johnson saw to it that the *Credo* was embraced by his company and urged his management to apply it as part of their everyday business philosophy.

J & J has obviously drawn heavily on the strength of these core values for guidance through the years, but at no time was this more evident than during the Tylenol crises of 1982 and 1986, when the product was adulterated with cyanide and used as a murder weapon. With its good name and reputation at stake, J & J company managers and employees made countless decisions that were inspired by the core values embodied in the *Credo*. The company's reputation was preserved, and business was regained.

To view a copy of the *Johnson & Johnson Credo* and some of the detailed history behind it, visit www.jnj.com. It's well worth the visit. And while you're at it, view the core values of the many other consistently profitable companies, such as 3M, as premier examples of the very strong correlation between values and profit.

The main lesson to be learned from the Johnson & Johnson scandal is that a morally sound, ethical, and practical set of values—fully imbedded in the company's culture—saves considerable time and consternation at times of periodic crisis, which occur in all businesses more than management would like to admit. It also minimizes fatal or near-fatal mistakes due to the absence of a philosophical base. Without clearly stated core values, questions like "What should we do?" and "What should our decisions be based on?" are open invitations to take the easy "answer of the moment" to address the immediate crises. Invariably, that easy answer ends up with dire consequences later on.

CULTURE

In his book, *Organizational Culture*, Edgar H. Schein describes *culture* as "A pattern of basic assumptions—invented, discovered, or developed by a given group as it learns to cope with its problems of external adaptation and internal integration—that has worked well enough to be considered valid and, therefore, to be taught to new members as the correct way to perceive, think and feel in relation to those problems."

Put another way, culture is a company's personality. Think of describing an acquaintance of yours to someone else. You might say things like, "She's very pleasant, very thoughtful of others, laughs a lot, and doesn't really take herself too seriously." Describing a company's culture is very much the same, but the definition obviously applies to a group of people collectively.

In a *Fortune* article entitled *It's the Business Model, Stupid*, Geoffrey Colvin mentioned that the best definition of culture he'd come across was this: "Culture is what people do when no one is telling them what to do."

A company's culture is really a part of, and should be a natural extension of, its core values, whose genesis, you'll recall from Part I, should be built on the philosophy that the key to a company's long-term success is the ability to attract, develop, and retain high-quality human talent. In this day and age, this talent is having an increasingly difficult time trying to balance work and personal demands. The increasing incidence of single heads of households, dual income families, and eldercare or childcare pressures are impacting all employees in all companies.

In a *Forbes* magazine article in November, 1996, entitled "When Money Isn't Enough", author Kerry Dolan put the ingredients of today's most effective cultures this way: "[Top firms] keep their all-important human talent by creating an atmosphere in which workers feel they are not mere factors of production, but organic elements of an enterprise that respects them and will bend itself to make their lives richer in ways that go beyond money."

Ms. Dolan went on to say,

> Millions of women have entered the work place—many of them struggle to balance career and family. More often men, too, are try-ing to strike bargains with employers in which money and titles are less important than intangible forms of reward—more time with family, for example, or a sense of control over their lives. Companies are increasingly looking at the psychological connections employees make with their employers and at whether they want their employ-ees to work grudgingly as wage slaves, or energetically and creatively as committed members of a team. To put it somewhat differently, workers want the workplace to take on some of the attributes of family life. You cannot assume that people can give all their priority to work. Companies need to legitimize and value their employees outside commitments in both the business and the human sense.

I believe that great companies treat their cultures as assets. Here's how we described RRI's culture:

This is how RRI's employees and service partners work together as a team and how prospective clients, employees, and service partners determine if there is a good mutual comfort zone:

A Progressive, Empowered Working Environment

RRI's culture encourages individual initiative, values diversity, allows for personal and professional growth, and fosters open communication and teamwork among all employees and service partners.

Informality and Trust

We don't stand on ceremony, formality, or bureaucracy—rather, we believe a relaxed, informal atmosphere, based on mutual trust, provides the best environment for continued growth and success.

Candid Communication

When communicating with our employees, clients, and service partners, we always attempt to "tell it the way it is" in a candid, straightforward manner.

Shared Vision

Our employees understand that in addition to their primary functions, they each play an important role in helping our company realize its broader strategic objectives. Further, they acknowledge that these shared, company-wide goals can only be realized through mutual respect for the strengths and opinions of all team members.

Quality Focus

We are committed to continually improving our level of service excellence so that it exceeds the constantly rising expectations of our clients and their transferees. At RRI, continuous process improvement (CPI) is based on the belief that there are always better ways to do what we do.

Correctly defining your organization's culture provides many, many benefits, not the least of which is that it will save you considerable time and aggravation trying to find ways to attract like-minded employees, clients, customers, and service partners.

You can't fake your culture. Employees and clients will quickly see through it. You are what you are, for better or worse. Ralph Waldo Emerson put it this way: "What you are thunders so loudly that I cannot hear what you say to the contrary."

Over the years I've been very surprised that many large companies don't make the effort to describe their cultures. In one such company I worked with over a period of time, I found the rank-and-file employees actually created and described their company's culture on their own, in the absence of any corporate-wide description. They described their company as "a rudderless ship headed out to sea with no destination in mind." By the way, that company eventually went the way of Chapter 11.

STRATEGY

Strategy is mostly the *how*—how you are going to fulfill your mission and achieve your vision. In his book *The Mind of the Strategist*, Kenichi Ohmae defines strategy as "creating sustaining values for the customer far better than those of competitors." He also said that "strategy starts with an ability to think in new and unconventional ways."

At RRI, our strategy was embodied in our *Performance Standards* for both corporate clients and their relocating employees. These were our essential "how to's," developed and refined over a long period of time. Here they are:

Client Performance Standards

Quite simply, RRI's unwavering objective is to provide a level of service excellence that our clients and their relocating employees can't get anywhere else. Here's how we deliver on that promise:

We earn our clients' trust and confidence in five key areas.

◈ We are consistently providing excellent service to their relocating employees (transferees).

◈ We are as responsive, knowledgeable, informative, innovative, and flexible in our relationships with our clients as we are with their transferees.

◈ We are always looking for ways to reduce our clients' costs without reducing service quality.

◈ We are consistently providing meaningful program information (in electronic and hard copy formats) and timely, accurate invoices.

◈ We are continually advising our clients on real estate and relocation matters that could impact their relocation policies and costs.

Transferee Performance Standards

We are committed to continually improving all facets of our organization—especially training, R & D, quality assurance, and information technology—to ensure the highest levels of transferee service satisfaction.

We help ease our transferees' stress of relocation by being:

◈ Responsive to our transferees' total relocation needs and prompt in responding to all communications.

◈ Knowledgeable in all aspects of relocation.

- ❖ Proactive, informing transferees about anything that could impact their relocation.
- ❖ Helpful and courteous in all our dealings with the transferee and his or her family.
- ❖ Innovative and flexible in finding solutions to our transferees' problems and concerns.

Maximizing Income/Minimizing Expenses

As mentioned earlier, strategy is the *how*—how you are going to fulfill your mission and achieve your vision. However, the *Performance Standards* described above won't be sustainable unless your organization is profitable, which comes from consistently maximizing income (through recognizing and exploiting opportunities both internally and externally) and minimizing expenses. Yes, one wasted paper clip, multiplied by X employees over X months...you get the idea.

Therefore, another key strategy is to get every last employee on the bandwagon of *consistently* looking for ways to maximize income and minimize expenses. Again, this requires the constant attention of the management staff from the CEO on down. The following e-mail from me to all employees will give you an example of how we stayed focused on this strategy:

To: All RRI Employees
From: Walt and Joe [*Joe Benevides was President/COO*]
Date: August 2, 1999
Subject: RRI Financial Update

Because most of our employees are RRI stockholders (and many more will join these ranks soon), I'm pleased to share with everyone an update of our financial condition.

Now that we've passed our half-year mark, we continue to be on target as to our 1999 profit objective with which you're all familiar.

However, two cautionary remarks are in order: 1) we normally derive well over half our revenue the last four months of our fiscal year, and 2) during this year of rapid growth, we must continue to watch our expenses very carefully as they can easily exceed that growth if we're not really careful.

Bottom line: we're having a good year—right on target, budgetwise. **As always, growth in profitability and the resultant value of your RRI stock is a direct reflection of all of us doing everything we possibly can to maximize income and minimize expense at every opportunity**—and we seem to be doing a great job in this regard while keeping our clients and their transferees happy with our service. As always, keep up the good work. We're pleased and proud to be associated with you.

—Walt and Joe

KEEPING YOUR FUNDAMENTAL BELIEFS ALIVE

I've learned that as an organization grows and prospers, it is imperative that ALL employees participate in the periodic review and refinement of all of the organization's fundamental beliefs. However, a word of caution: if and when you get to the point of being satisfied these fundamental beliefs are set in cement, give yourself a good kick in the pants and remind yourself that this is the time when you should really start worrying about your organization's future. My point is that in addition to the periodic necessity of revising some of your fundamental beliefs, you should always schedule regular reviews—at least once a year, in my experience.

Now, as for getting ALL employees to participate, you need to be patient, because consensus takes time. The way we approached the review was first, after the management staff had been fully advised in advance, as CEO I would e-mail our entire employee population and advise them of the review schedule. Each team would handle its own review meetings over the period of a month, and then representatives from each team would meet together, usually via teleconferencing, to compare notes and come up with a consensus. This was then forwarded to the Strategic Planning Team (the executive council, made up of the senior officers responsible for each company function). This way, over the years, there were very few instances when we didn't adopt all recommendations for revisions. In the few cases where we didn't adopt a recommendation, the president/COO or I would personally meet with the team representatives and explain why.

This was just one example of how we revised our fundamental beliefs to stay current and relevant, but our approach was always based on the same principle: people support what they help create.

PART II HIGHLIGHTS
POINTS TO REMEMBER

ON SERVICE
There's *service satisfaction* and then there's *service delight*. Service delight separates the winners from the mediocre. Winners clearly understand clients' and customers' real expectations and consistently exceed them.

SERVICE RECOVERY
Service foul-ups happen. When they do, it's imperative that the whole organization view them as an opportunity not only to recover, but to further cement the relationship.

ON SURVIVAL
Keep employees advised about negative happenings over which they have no control but that could have a negative impact on their jobs.

MISSION STATEMENT
The what, who, where, and why of your company.

VISION
The *where*, as in, "Where are we going?"

CORE VALUES
The philosophical convictions guiding the organization on a successful journey.

VALUES/PROFITABILITY
There is a direct relationship.

CULTURE
The company's collective personality. A natural extension of core values. Having a clearly stated culture saves considerable time in attracting like-minded employees, clients, customers, and service partners.

KEEPING FUNDAMENTAL BELIEFS ALIVE
It's imperative that all employees participate in periodic review and refinement—whether or not the executive staff feels it is warranted.

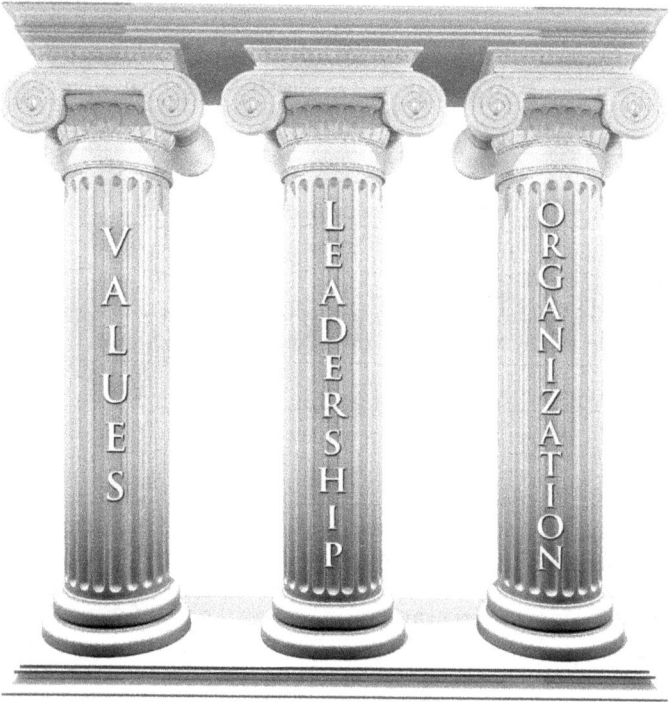

PART III

Values Applied

THE GLOBAL ECONOMY IS KNOWLEDGE INTENSIVE

"The world is becoming not labor intensive, not material intensive, not energy intensive, but knowledge intensive." (Peter Drucker, *The Age of Discontinuity*).

I have believed this for years, and related this belief to practice based on the principle that the only sustainable competitive advantage left for any organization is the quality of human talent. And whereas the demand for knowledge workers is projected to far exceed the supply, the key to business success in the twenty-first century will be to recruit, develop, and retain this high-quality human talent.

Now, in this section of the book, it's time to put theory into practice—to build on the foundation of your fundamental beliefs.

Managing knowledge in the contemporary business world is just as important as managing money. Successful companies of the future will clearly be seen as learning organizations. Peter Senge defined *learning organizations* in his book, *The Fifth Discipline*, as "a group of people who are continually enhancing their capability to create their own future."

In this section, we'll explore the key ingredients that go into the mix of creating a culture that will maximize the critical tasks of recruiting, developing, and retaining human talent, and accelerating the knowledge of those humans through organizational learning.

HUMAN RESOURCES (HR) FUNDAMENTALS

If you are the founder or CEO of your company, or the leader of your team or division, one of the most fundamental of all HR issues is the philosophical foundation through which you view your employees in the work environment you desire. In this regard, the teachings of two management gurus come to mind. In his classic book *The Human Side of Enterprise*, Douglas McGregor says, in essence, that in what he describes as a theory Y business environment employees are viewed as people who can be trusted, who want to do the right thing, and who are capable of imagination and ingenuity. Conversely, in a theory X environment, employees are viewed as inherently lazy, needing to be supervised and motivated, and regarding work as necessary only to provide money. McGregor suggests these two theories are on a continuum, and says that the style of management of all organizations obviously falls somewhere in that continuum. There is no doubt in my mind that the far end of the theory Y side of the continuum is the way to go in the twenty-first century.

In the other classic, *One More Time: How Do You Motivate Employees?*, Frederick Herzberg contends that true employee motivation comes from achievement, personal development, job satisfaction, and recognition, not money, per se. He believes that the objective should be to motivate employees through the job itself rather than through rewards and pressure. I wholeheartedly agree.

A Strategic Function

Another fundamental is the role of the human resources department—how it's viewed by, and operates within, the organization. Based on my philosophy that the only sustainable competitive advantage left to the business world is the quality of human talent and knowledge, it should be obvious that I believe that HR is just as important as all the other functions and, in many cases, more so, and should have a place of importance at the strategic planning table.

At RRI, our HR group was a key player in the development and ongoing refinement of all our fundamental beliefs, including our core values. While other major functions of the company spent time focusing on the outside world, HR spent its time inside, constantly checking the pulse of our culture and morale, which we viewed as its number one job.

Accordingly, when important decisions had to be made, our President/ COO Joe Benevides and I would use HR as a sounding board. As a result, we could always predict how our employees would react so we could develop our plan and approach accordingly. As detailed later in this book, when we had to have pay cuts and work reductions due to the 9/11 tragedy, both Joe and I received notes and e-mails from over 60 percent of our employees conveying that they understood and appreciated our honesty about the situation and asking how they could help.

All the HR philosophies and practices in the world aren't worth a hill of beans unless the top leaders of the company set the tone and walk the talk 100 percent—even better, 200 percent.

Diversity

Diversity is another HR fundamental. In a global economy, workforce diversity is not an option, it's a must. Diverse gender, race, age, and cultural background reflect the world and, therefore, for many companies, their customers, clients, service partners, and employees. Top companies understand that their culture must embrace diversity and tolerance, and therefore, the only selection criteria is this: given that the candidate has the qualifications, how does the employer ensure this individual will thrive within the company's culture?

I had the great pleasure of spending considerable time with Proctor & Gamble (P & G), who was one of our major international services clients. They had (and I'm sure have to this day) a very strong commitment to funding and helping diverse, minority individuals and organizations start or expand businesses and sought my advice on real estate and global employee mobility operations. Their commitment—which reflected their market—was global in nature.

When I first learned of this initiative, I was skeptical, particularly about the large sums of money P & G was committed to investing in this program. However, as my involvement and awareness grew, I came to realize how truly strategic and intelligent this commitment was. The global market is huge and diverse and will increasingly impact the bottom line of all the multi-nationals and many other companies.

The main lesson I took away from this experience is this: diverse and/or minority segments of the global population form a significant block of tomorrow's consumers and will identify with products and companies they view as tolerant and compatible with their particular diversity or minority status.

Steve Reinemund, CEO of PepsiCo put it this way: "It would seem obvious that if we don't have people from the frontline up to the boardroom who represent the consumers we sell to, we're not going to be successful."

Age: Preference or Discrimination?

Over the years, some of the most productive employees I worked with were in their eighties and had been employed for more than twenty years.

In the workforce environment of the 21st Century—where the demand for knowledge workers will exceed supply—mandatory retirement ages are counterproductive.

The signs are everywhere. Check any industry and you will find workers who retired in their sixties being called back time and again on a consulting basis, which invariably costs the company far more than the pay/benefit level of the employees before retirement.

My philosophy was this: provided our seniors 1) could climb the stairs to our office building (even on an assisted basis), 2) maintained their mental acuity, and 3) kept up with the times, their knowledge and experience were well worth every penny of their salaries and benefits.

I should point out that these seniors were in positions that did not require a great deal of physical stamina—let the younger tigers handle on-the-road sales and service jobs.

RECRUITING/SELECTING

Another key HR issue is to know precisely what you are looking for and the most effective way to know when you've found it. All the wonderful or horrible things that can happen to an organization start with the recruiting and selection processes; they're distinct but inseparably connected activities. It all starts there. Successful organizations understand and apply this principle consistently.

At RRI, here's how we described the ideal employee: self-directed, open-minded, professional, a team player, reliable, career-minded, flexible, and adaptive to constant change. In other words, we knew these were the key attributes required for someone to be comfortable and productive in our culture.

Utopian, you say? Not during the last ten years of RRI's life, when we were considered the industry's employer of choice for top professionals. We had no real recruitment expenses because we had a continuous pipeline of quality job candidates. Obviously, it was not always that way. In the earlier years we had to spend our share of recruitment dollars and settle for some employees with less than 100 percent of our ideals—but not much less, because we knew what we were looking for.

The next logical question that comes to mind is, how do you go about determining whether the candidate has what you're looking for? Over and above the normal approaches (talking with prior employers, checking references, and determining technical skills), our approach involved considerable time and people.

After an HR representative conducted the first interview, if the rep felt the process should continue, he or she would very thoroughly review our mission, vision, core values, and culture, with particular emphasis on the last two. Then a spontaneous tour of the office would follow, with random stops to chat with different staff in different jobs, encouraging the applicant to ask honest and frank questions. Our HR rep would stress, throughout this first interview, that our culture was not for everyone, and it was to the benefit of both parties to try to determine the likelihood of a mutual comfort zone up front.

One of the last subjects discussed at the conclusion of this first interview (if the HR rep felt the candidate should continue the selection process) was our philosophy of mutual expectations (see page 65).

The HR rep would point out that before the next series of interviews, the candidate should very carefully review these mutual expectations and make sure that he or she was comfortable with both the company and employee expectations—and ask questions or air any concerns at the beginning of the next series of interviews.

Mutual Expectations

RRI believes that the key to its success is a reciprocal, balanced level of expectations between the company and each of its employees.

What employees can expect from RRI:

- A competitive compensation and comprehensive benefits package and employee policies that balance work and family responsibilities.

- The opportunity to become owners/stockholders of the company.

- Honesty in advising about corporate objectives and the current and projected viability of the company.

- Strong leadership that can maintain RRI's growth so that employees have job security and further career opportunities.

- Opportunities for personal growth and advancement based strictly on merit and qualifications.

- A working environment that encourages individual initiative, allows for personal professional growth, and fosters open communication and teamwork among all employees.

- Commitment to diversity among our employee staff and the fair treatment of all employees.

- A clean, professional, safe, and pleasant working environment, including the most progressive tools necessary to perform the job.

- Training that will help employees perform their jobs better and broaden their career growth opportunities.

- Employee performance that will be evaluated fairly.

Mutual Expectations *(continued)*

What RRI expects from employees:

- That they understand and appreciate that the key to RRI's success is consistently exceeding our clients' service and cost expectations.

- That they are open-minded, flexible, and adaptive, understanding that change is a constant of our competitive marketplace.

- That they are honest and forthright in communicating their ideas and concerns.

- That they are self-directed, professional, reliable, career-oriented team players.

- That when scheduling Paid Time Off (PTO), employees take into consideration the needs of fellow team members and RRI's clients and transferees.

- That they understand their responsibility as company owners, doing everything possible to maximize revenue and minimize expenses.

- That they have a willingness to continually broaden their knowledge and skills.

- That they respect RRI's request for confidentiality in specified matters.

- That they treat RRI's service partners and each other with dignity and respect, regardless of work performed or job level.

- That they help RRI remain a respected corporate citizen in the communities where its employees work and live.

Mutual Expectations

I believe that in relationships of every nature, including marriage, partnerships, joint ventures, and service contracts between clients and suppliers, the incidence of relationship failure can be traced in large part to the failure of the two parties to clearly understand and appreciate mutual expectations —what each side expects of the other—before they shake hands, sign a contract, or say "I do."

The employer/employee relationship certainly should fall into this category. In fact, outside the family, that relationship represents the greatest number of people involved. Yet I have found that very few businesses have taken the time or have the inclination to establish employer/employee mutual expectations. What a shame for both parties.

For many years, I believed the primary social contract between United States employers and their employees could be characterized as "show up for work, be reliable, and do your job—it's yours for life, and the company will take care of you when you retire." I witnessed, first-hand, the erosion of this long-standing social contract starting in the mid-eighties. Three of the bellwethers that I would periodically benchmark in this regard were senior HR executives at Eastman Kodak, DuPont, and General Mills.

It was interesting, if not a bit painful, to hear them tell me how they were grappling with the necessity of breaking this long-standing (but unspoken) social contract. It's also interesting to note that it was at about the same time that the competitive pressures of the global economy were beginning to be felt in the United States. As a result, things were beginning to move to a performance and quality orientation regarding how a company viewed its fundamental relationship with its employees.

The preamble to the RRI statement of *Mutual Expectations* is important: "RRI believes that the key to its success is a reciprocal, balanced level of expectations between the company and each of its employees." Note that both the employee and RRI expectations total ten each and take approximately the same amount of space (and time) to convey. Everything balanced equally, always.

One of the major areas of candidate analysis was maturity, both in age and job experience. We found that if applicants had very little or no prior job experience, it was difficult for them to evaluate what we felt was the real quality of our work environment. They had nothing to compare it to. We learned this over the years, when first-time job candidates joined us, left a few years later, then came back rather quickly, telling us, in essence, that they never appreciated how good they had it at RRI. Once they came back with this attitude and we rehired them, I don't know of one who didn't then stay to make it a long-term career.

After this first interview and tour with the HR rep, if both parties wanted to continue, the HR rep would tell the candidate that she or he would be in touch to schedule a series of interviews, stressing our philosophy that we viewed interviewing as a two-way street, i.e., we expected them to interview us as much as we interviewed them. Typically, the first interview in this series would be with the candidate's potential manager (who made the final hiring decision), followed by a good cross-section of three or four management and non-management employees that HR thought would provide a good, balanced assessment. All feedback flowed back through the HR rep to the manager. There were a few occasions over the years when a particular manager didn't hit if off with a candidate who everyone else thought was great, in which case every effort was made to match that candidate with another manager.

I should stress that we learned over time that our culture was particularly ideal for people with a sense of humor who were very comfortable in an informal atmosphere. That essentially was the constant that all the non-HR interviewers were looking for. This was fairly easy to ascertain through our approach of two or more multiple interview sessions over a two- or three-week period. The higher the job level or responsibility, the more extended the number of interviews and time.

CAREER DEVELOPMENT

In my experience, successful companies see career development as an investment, not a chore. We certainly did, and that development starts on day one with a comprehensive new employee orientation, the first step in a continuing education program.

Reflecting our view that career development is a major investment and asset, our continuing education program was very comprehensive: we offered seven courses in our fundamental (100-series) program, including such topics as "About RRI/Industry," "Global Relocation Fundamentals," and "Diversity in the Workplace."

The ongoing courses in our 200 series delved into more specific topics such as "RRI Global Capabilities (Basic and Advanced)," "The Relocation Process (Basic and Advanced)," and "HR Fundamentals for Managers."

We also had special courses that offered general, 300-series subjects such as "Mortgage Basics," "The Moving Industry," and "Handling Difficult Client and Transferee Situations"; 400-series consulting group courses like "Relocation Best Practices" and "Global Tax Issues"; and outside trainers (500 Series) courses on writing and presentation skills.

We had three distinct curricula for management, professional staff, and administrative staff.

Continuing education programs of this nature must of course be tailored to the industry and the unique company.

Wholesale or Retail Training?

Because our recruitment needs were not concentrated within certain time frames, we viewed our training needs as "retail" in nature—that is, one at a time. This means there was no way we could rationalize a full-time training staff. So we had "visiting faculty," employee volunteers approved by our career development department, a division of HR, specified for different subjects. The new employee, after his or her first day spent with HR, would spend the rest of the first week or two with various visiting faculty members addressing all those courses in the 100 series. All feedback was provided to HR and then reported to the candidate's manager.

Cross-Functional Training

We believed that in virtually every organization, all functions and activities ultimately relate to and impact one another. For example, if a client gets an incorrect bill from the finance department, it immediately impacts that client's relationship manager on a service team. Thus, we also created what we called "cross-functional training," wherein the candidate, after completing the fundamentals series, was scheduled to spend time with peers in all the other functional areas of the company. The peer trainers enjoyed explaining their teams' functions, activities, and challenges and how they interrelated with the candidate's job and the rest of the company.

Promote from Within

We wanted our leaders and future leaders to be like family members, people who had experienced some of the growth challenges of the company and had a firsthand feel for the culture and breadth of the organization, including services, staff, and the different geographic markets we served. There is no better career development than providing personal growth opportunities for those who excel at whatever task they undertake and continually strive to broaden their knowledge and skills.

Evolution of Employee Quality

As an organization continues to grow over the years, it is logical that the quality of the employee population will grow and improve on a parallel path. Every growing organization faces this phenomenon and the challenge of what to do with the dedicated, loyal employees left behind. These are the employees who find themselves in the same position today that they have been in for some time. The performance objectives and scope of work have upgraded considerably over time, but their capabilities have not.

Here's what we did in a situation like this: after consulting with HR, the employees' managers would sit down with the employees to discuss the problem, which, by the way, was rarely a surprise to these employees. They knew full well they were in over their head whether or not they admitted it, and certainly the employees' other team members were well aware of the problem.

If we felt the employee could remain a positive, contributing asset to the company in another (usually lower) position, we would assist that employee in making the move to that position and saving face with his or her peers. In office communications, for example, we might say, "After nine years with the company in the same position, Mary and the company felt it was time for a change which would broaden her knowledge of the company and help her continue to enhance her career path at RRI. Accordingly, she's become a candidate for a relocation administrator position on Sally's team."

If the employee was retained, we would never reduce his or her current pay level. Typically, the employee was not at the top level of the applicable pay grade, so we would make every effort to match current pay at the top of the lesser grade level with the understanding that the salary would remain static (no increases considered) until all salary levels were changed company-wide.

On the other hand, if we felt the employee did not have the likelihood of being a dedicated, contributing employee in any capacity in the future, we would terminate that employee on the grounds that he or she was not meeting personal performance objectives.

RETENTION

So, you now have invested considerable resources in recruiting, selecting, and developing your high-quality human talent. Talented employees have brought good knowledge with them and are constantly adding to organizational knowledge, thus helping your company stay ahead of the competition. The question now is, how do you keep them in the family? Following are several approaches and concepts that have worked very well for me over the years.

The Culture

There is no doubt in my mind that in the very best companies, the primary retention motivator is the company's culture itself. Assuming we had done our work correctly, we knew there was a good comfort zone with the employee when hired.

Looking forward to going to work every day with the people you like, at a company you are proud to be a part of, and performing the work you really enjoy in an exciting, positive work environment is, of and by itself, the most powerful retention vehicle.

Meaningful Work

If your employees feel there is a truly meaningful, worthwhile rationale for the work they do, they will gain so much more—and, therefore, so will your company. A number of years ago, I tackled this issue at RRI. The following e-mail message to all employees describes our process of coming up with a phrase to describe our work. It proved over the years to be well worth periodically reiterating at company town meetings, in company update reports, and at general group or team meetings.

However, like many company-wide initiatives, it can become out of sight, out of mind. In my estimation, the key to all employee programs of any nature is sustainability. Develop a plan concurrently with the new program that will assure you it will be sustained over the desired period of time. In this case, that period of time was indefinite.

To: All RRI Employees
From: Walt
Date: September 14, 2000
Subject: "We Ease the Stress of Relocation"

Back in August, at the conclusion of the Employee Appreciation Day company meeting, I solicited your input in developing a phrase that clearly conveys the importance and meaningfulness of what we all do at RRI every day.

As you can imagine, I received many terrific ideas, which I have been reviewing with our communications department.

"We Ease the Stress of Relocation" is our choice, which reflects a combination of suggestions. Further, we have decided to highlight some of the specific employee suggestions we received in future editions of the *RRI Insider* and *Clients' Update* publications.

FYI, the following is the preface we will be using to introduce specific employee suggestions: "Relocation can be exciting: a challenging new assignment; a different city to explore; a new home to enjoy; and friends to be made. Relocation can also be enormously difficult: starting a new position is invariably demanding; selling an old residence and finding a new one can be a formidable task; and leaving friends and family behind is hard. It's not surprising that psychologists identify relocation as one of life's most stressful experiences. Because RRI employees feel that what they do to minimize this stress is important and meaningful, it shows in the quality of service we provide relocating employees and their families, as well as our clients."

—Walt

Pay and Benefits

If you have an effective, attractive culture, your pay scale can be competitive as opposed to very competitive. Put another way, if your organization is having trouble hiring or keeping the type of employee you really want, chances are your pay scale—as well as your benefits—is not competitive or is competitive but your culture needs refinement.

Your benefits must reflect your core values and culture. In this regard, you have to put your money where your mouth is. For example, in *Mutual Expectations* we said that "employees can expect employee policies that balance work and personal/family responsibilities."

We were well aware of the contemporary pressures of dual income families, single heads of household, eldercare, and childcare. Therefore, one of the very competitive benefits we offered our employees was reflected in our PTO (paid time off) policy, which stated:

Time may be used for any purpose: vacation, illness, or personal. Beginning with next calendar year from date of hire:

Up to 4 years: 4 weeks PTO (20 business days)

Over 4 years, but less than 9 years: 5 weeks PTO (25 business days)

Over 9 years: 6 weeks PTO (30 business days)

This policy was one of the key benefits cementing a loyal and committed workforce, because we truly put our money where our mouth was. As we stated in our core values, our promise was to provide "employee policies that address the contemporary challenges of balancing work and personal demands."

I'm sure that many readers at first blush will question how we could run a successful company with this much time off available to the employee population, particularly when we had a large percentage of employees who had worked with us for over nine years. Frankly, it was never a problem, because these loyal, committed employees managed their time off like responsible adults and members of the team, and the incidence of misuse was minor. Additionally, this policy virtually eliminated troublesome unscheduled absences, which was one of the goals.

In *Mutual Expectations*, we asked that "when scheduling paid time off (PTO), employees take into consideration the needs of fellow team members and RRI's clients and transferees."

We also made sure our pay scale was competitive; that is, that it was pretty much the average for comparable jobs in the same labor market. We would hire an independent survey group to survey companies similar to ours every year to make sure our wages were still fair. We always shared the results of this survey with all our employees. Equally important, we shared our entire salary structure—from the lowest level exempt positions to mine as CEO—with our entire employee family. There were no hidden secrets regarding any aspect of the organization.

In addition, all staff members with a manager, director, or officer designation were eligible for an annual bonus ranging from 10 percent to 20 percent of their annual salary. Up to half of this bonus was based on personal performance objectives while up to another half was based on levels of company pre-tax margin. For example, if we hit a 15 percent margin and above, the full 50 percent would apply; if less than 15 percent, the 50 percent would be ratcheted downward.

The bottom line on pay and benefits is that if you have an effective culture, you can and should be competitive. If you don't, and you want to upgrade the quality of your staff, you must be very competitive. Benefits must reflect your integrated core values, culture, and mutual expectations.

Getting the Benefit from Benefits

The caliber of human talent your organization will attract and retain will appreciate if you offer a package of comprehensive pay and benefits that reflect your culture and core values. However, after a certain period of time, employees may forget how good they have it—in other words, out of sight, out of mind.

All by way of saying, if you've got it, flaunt it; at the least, keep your attractive pay and benefits package in the forefront of your employees' minds. My definition of PR is "doing good and getting credit for it." If your benefits package is good, make sure your employees know about and appreciate it, and that the company is getting credit for it...consistently.

There are several ways to go about this. One way is to do what we did at RRI: at least once a year we would share with our entire employee family the facts about how our salary structure and benefits stacked up with our industry, in comparable industries, and in the local labor market. Another, and probably more effective, way came about quite naturally as new recruits began telling their peers when they came on board that our salary and benefits package was the best in the industry.

Recognition Programs

At the beginning of this section, I summarized the philosophy of Frederick Herzberg from the *Harvard Business Review* classic, *One More Time: How Do You Motivate Employees?* True employee motivation comes from achievement, personal development, job satisfaction, and recognition. All revolve around the job; thus, motivation should come from the job itself, not pay, per se.

Recognition is obviously a very important component of motivation. However, the age-old problem for most companies is sustainability, i.e., how do you keep an employee recognition program fresh and viable throughout its desired life cycle?

What worked for our company (after much trial and error) was this process: 1) Once the idea for the program starts to take shape and HR believes it may have merit, be sure to get input from a broad sampling of the entire employee population before making a "go" or "no go" decision. 2) If response is positive, appoint a representational employee task force that works with HR to put the finishing touches on the program (task force members must get input from their operating team members). 3) When the program is finalized, go back to the task force and request they concurrently develop a plan to assure that the program will be sustained at the desired level of participation during its desired life cycle.

A summary of our recognition programs is reproduced below. The key features of sustainability were the "POP (Power of Partnering) Quarterly Grand Prize." The many POP Certificates visible throughout the company, and the constant publicizing of the various program participants in our *RRI News* Intranet program and at company-wide meetings and town hall meetings encouraged other employees to strive to be similarly recognized.

Recognition Programs

In order to recognize exceptional contributions and performance by RRI's employees, the human resources department has developed three distinct employee recognition programs:

Power of Partnering

This program gives employees the opportunity to formally thank and acknowledge fellow employees when help is provided by that employee beyond his/her normal job responsibilities, e.g., extra effort to help a fellow employee.

Any employee can grant a "Power of Partnering" acknowledgement for a fellow employee at any time, following the instructions in the nomination form. (Please hit the Escape key on your PC to view the nomination form and proceed with the nomination.) The system will automatically complete the Power of Partnering certificate (see page 79), which can then be printed by the person making the acknowledgement who then signs, dates, and personally delivers it to the recipient.

Also, the system automatically copies HR so that the recipient can be included in the POP quarterly grand prize drawing and to the communications department for insertion in *RRI News* (see below). Quarterly, all recipient names will be combined for the chance to win the POP quarterly grand prize drawing, which is an AMEX gift certificate of $500. Multiple names on one award will be entered in the quarterly raffle individually. The highlights of all recipients and their partnering efforts will be described in the next *RRI News*.

Creative Solution

This program is a way for management to recognize employees whose ideas increase revenue and/or efficiencies that control or reduce expenses.

As part of their job, everyone at RRI should always be looking for ways to improve the quality and efficiency of work in her/his area. The elimination of redundancies and duplications are givens, as is finding ways to communicate with one's workplace constituency.

⌂RRI

Power of
Partnering
Award

This Certificate Recognizes

Name

as an employee who exemplifies the
power of employee-to-employer partnering.

Thanks for your extra effort in helping me out.

February 11, 2004
Date

Recognized by **Name**

RRI Chairman/CEO

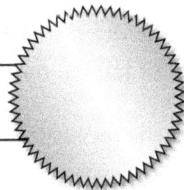

Over and above these expectations that go with the job, the Creative Solution Award recognizes an idea that results in a totally new revenue opportunity and/or a truly breakthrough efficiency not recognized by management.

Following the instructions provided in the nomination form, the nominating manager will describe the employee's Creative Solution, detailing the expense/revenue benefits projected to be derived from such a solution. This is forwarded to the appropriate division head.

If approved by the division head, he/she will specify the dollar amount of the award.

HR will order a trophy commemorating the award, and then the manager will present the trophy and monetary award to the employee in a group or team meeting setting—highlighting the achievement.

The creative solution will be featured in *RRI News*.

Above and Beyond

This program is a way for management to recognize an employee whose extra effort justifies personal recognition and a monetary reward.

Following the instructions provided in the nomination form, the nominating manager will describe the extra effort of the employee involved and recommend a specific monetary figure.

The award and the monetary amount must be approved by the vice president of human resources.

If approved, the nominating manager will present the monetary award to the employee either in a group or personal setting, at the manager's discretion.

The story may be described in *RRI News* if the nominating manager feels it is appropriate.

Communication

You will recall that one of the key aspects of our culture was candid communication. We said, "When communicating with our employees, clients, and preferred service partners, we always attempt to 'tell it the way it is' in a candid, straightforward manner."

Trust goes to the heart of building and maintaining a quality organization of high-quality human talent. Trust comes from honesty on a long-term, consistent basis. Once again, *consistent* is the key word because with just one misstep, trust can be quickly lost and, once lost, can only be won back slowly.

We put it this way in our *Mutual Expectations*, under the heading "What employees can expect from RRI": "Honesty in advising about corporate objectives and the current and projected economic viability of the company."

These philosophies guided us in all our employee relations and communications. No one has a problem conveying good news; however, communicating bad news is another matter. Many managers vacillate and procrastinate and/or try to sugarcoat bad news, which only makes matters worse later on.

As an example of a straight-on approach to communicating some really bad news to our entire employee family, you'll find a company-wide e-mail message below that was distributed shortly after the 9/11 tragedy that brought our business to a stand-still.

To: All RRI Employees
From: Walt and Joe [*Joe Benevides was President/COO*]
Date: September 19, 2001
Subject: Response to Reduced Activity/Revenue

As you are all aware, RRI, like many corporations, has seen a decline in volume and revenue during recent months. This situation has become even more serious since last Tuesday's devastating terrorist attack on the United States.

Our industry depends on corporate willingness to deploy employees freely to achieve their objectives. Understandably, many of our clients are proceeding cautiously in this uncertain time. Many companies were acting to control expenses even before last week's tragedy, and today they are even more reluctant to engage in travel and mobility activities unless absolutely necessary.

We are gathering more information on our clients' thoughts and plans, and our hope is that this slowdown is a short-term phenomenon. Ultimately, we firmly believe that most clients and prospects will continue to find employee mobility to be an important tool to achieve their business objectives.

In the meantime, we are forced to take several actions that will allow us to bring RRI's expenses in line with our reduced revenues while retaining our ability to provide the highest level of client and transferee service.

1. For a five-week period, from October 1 through November 2, all **non-management** workweeks and compensation will be reduced by 10 percent, and **management's** will be reduced by 20 percent. Both of us will take pay reductions of 25 percent. During these three pay periods, benefits will not be affected by this action; all remain at full-time levels.

   Please note: in select service-related departments with currently high levels of transferees in process, implementation of this plan may be delayed to mitigate any negative impact on service levels.

2. Additionally, internal company travel is suspended for the balance of the fiscal year. However, travel at the request of a prospect or client, or to attend previously arranged and paid-for industry meetings, is excluded.

3. We are continuing to review all other discretionary expenses and will make reductions wherever possible.

We are well aware of the hardship that this action will cause and our HR group is prepared to assist you in any way possible. For example, you may elect to terminate your 401K contributions. Additionally, HR is exploring the opportunity to supplement these reduced wages through unemployment compensation. Your manager will be receiving further details on these options from HR.

These are difficult times, and we appreciate your continued loyalty and support. Again, our hope is that volume and business confidence will rebound soon. We will continue to monitor the situation closely and keep you informed. Please contact your manager if you have any questions.

In the meantime, we know you join with us in extending our deepest sympathies to those who lost loved ones on 9/11.

—Walt and Joe

As mentioned earlier, we received feedback on this e-mail from over 60 percent of our employees. The consistent message was, "Thanks for being honest. We certainly don't like this, but we understand why it's necessary. How can we help?"

Unfortunately, on November 1 we had to advise our employees that activity and revenue had not rebounded. In fact, they had further deteriorated, and we were forced, for the first time in our history, to reduce our workforce throughout the company by approximately 7 to 9 percent. Even with our great company/employee relations, we were surprised that we got feedback similar in nature to the first e-mail from nearly 70 percent of our employees.

One reason for this positive reaction to negative news was what Lee Iacocca referred to as "equality of sacrifice" in his autobiography. Everyone in the company—from the CEO on down—took the hit, at least equally on a percentage basis.

Meetings

Meetings are an important form of organizational communication, but can be, and often are, misused. Over the years, I came to the following conclusions about meetings, in general.

First, as everyone in a management position could schedule and conduct meetings as part of our continuing education program, they were required to attend and successfully complete the course entitled "How to Prepare and Conduct Productive Meetings."

The key aspects of this training were focused on the need for the person responsible for the meeting to 1) clearly state the objective of the meeting beforehand and, like all educational objectives, specify clearly what the attendees should know after the meeting that they didn't know before the meeting. 2) Develop a way to find out if this objective had been met. 3) Always start precisely at the time specified (no matter if you are the only one in the room), and never go beyond the ending time. 4) Learn and practice how to outline a meeting—that is, prepare a productive agenda in the time scheduled.

This approach to agenda development came from my experience in planning and conducting literally thousands of meetings and conferences. Over the years, when confronted with trying to explain an idea or present something to a group, I had developed the habit of mentally outlining that idea with the basic interrogatives *what, why,* and *how.* If I had to go on and explain further, I'd usually throw in the *when* and *where* as well. So, this discipline of how to approach agenda development was included in our training curriculum and proved to be very helpful to the management staff.

My second major conclusion was that you had to have a practical policy on maximum meeting times and times of day to avoid the potential of murder by meeting and losing sight of why we were there; that is, to service our corporate clients and their relocating employees and families.

For employees who didn't interface with clients and/or transferees, the maximum meeting time during established business hours was sixty minutes. For those who did interface with clients and/or transferees, the time allotted was thirty minutes. In either case, there was no more than one meeting a week. So if managers in the service function felt they needed to schedule a one-hour meeting, they would frequently start the meeting at either thirty minutes before opening time or thirty minutes before closing time or, on occasion, look for volunteers to schedule half the attendees during part of the lunch hour and the rest at either of the above described meetings.

There were occasions, of course, when management needed to "blue sky" ideas and strategic plans, in which event we'd schedule after hours break-aways or weekend retreats away from the office. These typically had no specific (or very loose) agendas but, as always, we required meeting objectives specifying what we wanted to accomplish. For example, "Should we rethink our marketing and sales strategy and if so, how should it be changed?" It's important to point out that to be most effective, this type of meeting needs an effective facilitator—someone who can keep the meeting moving, get everyone involved by asking open-ended "why and how" questions, and not interpose his or her own opinions.

My comments on communication wouldn't be complete without me sharing with you some background on a communication vehicle we found very effective, and that was the town hall meeting. At least once a year, and often several times a year if special situations warranted, Joe Benevides and/or I would personally conduct a meeting with all the staff of each office. These meetings typically lasted no more than thirty minutes.

After coordinating with the office manager, our HR department would e-mail everyone in the office advising them when the meeting was scheduled, informing them of the subjects to be discussed, and soliciting their questions in advance.

The subjects we prepared to discuss were usually the same: update of significant events that had recently transpired (inside and outside the company); current status of activity and budget; status of our vision achievement; and projection of what we saw as major challenges and opportunities that lay ahead. (We called this the "yesterday, today, and tomorrow" approach.)

With regard to soliciting their questions in advance, HR and our information technology (IT) group set up an anonymous e-mail system so that, if certain employees were concerned about anonymity, they would not be identified with the question they had asked. Additionally, all employees were advised that we would, of course, also take questions from the floor.

I remember one such meeting when one of the advance, anonymous questions stated: "Walter, as CEO of the company, why don't you forego all your pay and benefits during this post-9/11 phase we're going through?"

At the meeting, I handled this just like all the other questions, by reading them verbatim and answering as best I could. In this case my answer was, "Believe it or not, I too have ongoing financial obligations, and taking a 25 percent hit is going to hurt me as much as I'm sure your 10 percent hit will hurt you."

Here's the interesting upshot of this one meeting: right after it concluded, I was swamped by the majority of the employees in that office whose message was essentially, "We are so embarrassed that someone in this office would ask such a dumb, rude question. It certainly doesn't reflect the sentiments of the rest of us."

We always addressed all questions without exception or edits because in so doing we perpetuated and reinforced some of our most fundamental beliefs, including the fact that we believed in "telling it like it is."

As described elsewhere in this book, trust and loyalty take a long time to develop, but once instilled throughout the organization, they go to the heart of leadership and the building of a great organization. One of the most important ways to instill that trust and loyalty is to always walk the talk.

Checking the Morale Pulse

RRI was a geographically diversified organization with five offices in the United States, one in Canada, and one in England. We had a total of 375 employees, over 2,000 RRI-trained accredited representatives in the United States, and 850 global accredited representatives in 110 countries.

As we grew, we felt the need to regularly assess how well we were communicating and living up to our core values, culture, and the company side of mutual expectations. As a result, we came up with six key questions, the answers to which we felt would give us a true gauge on how well we were doing on a company-wide basis. Here are the questions:

- ❖ In your opinion, to what extent do you feel you know the general purpose and objectives of all the company's major functions?

- ❖ In your opinion, to what extent do you have an understanding of the major company initiatives currently being pursued and planned for the future?

- ❖ In your opinion, to what extent do you feel RRI provides you with the flexibility to both balance and meet the requirements of your work and personal/family life?

- ❖ To what extent do you plan to commit to investing in a long-term career with RRI?

- ❖ In your opinion, to what extent do you feel RRI communicates with you in a candid, straightforward manner?

- ❖ In your opinion, to what extent do you feel RRI encourages individual initiative, values diversity, allows for personal and professional growth, and fosters open communication and teamwork among all employees?

Employees were asked to respond to each question as follows: 1 (not at all); 2 (to some extent); 3 (to a moderate extent); 4 (to a great extent); or 5 (to a very great extent). The survey was conducted twice a year by e-mail to all employees who responded on an anonymous basis.

The results of our second survey are reproduced below, and you'll note that we obviously had found a way, between the first and second survey, to get desired participation. It's that sustainability issue again.

The bottom line is this: anything worth doing is worth doing well *and* measuring the results. Finding out if your core values, culture, and employee expectations are being met—or trending up or down—is certainly worth measuring.

To: All RRI Employees
From: Walt and Joe
Date: January 21, 2003
Subject: Results of Employee Opinion Survey

You will find the results of our recent Employee Opinion Survey attached. Overall, a score of 3.88 was achieved, up a bit from last June's score of 3.58. Generally speaking, it appears we still need to do a better job of communication throughout the company if we are to reach our objective of achieving a score of no less than 4.00.

The number of participants in our fourth Employee Opinion Survey showed a marked improvement over those from June 2002. We were able to increase the participation from a mere 69 percent in June up to 93 percent for the December survey. Thank you for your participation.

One office actually met the company-established target rating of 4.00 on 50 percent of the survey questions. We are very pleased about this and look forward to similar results for all offices.

Additionally, 23.2 percent of the respondents elaborated with comments on this December survey as compared to our June survey in which only 15 percent added comments. Furthermore, the break between positive and negative remarks was nearly evenly split. Almost 92 percent of the positive comments are tied directly to the overall view of the company as "a great place to work". The remainder of the positive comments related to communication and training initiatives.

From a negative perspective, nearly 43 percent of those comments related to a lack of career growth and management opportunities within RRI. Frankly, this is not surprising. Coming off the two worst years in our industry's history, career growth and management opportunities have been static at best throughout the industry.

On another note, there were a few negatives about a lack of team spirit/communication across company lines. In light of these comments, we have discussed possible training initiatives with our management staff which we are confident will address these concerns.

Once again, thanks so much for your participation—it really helps us to know what has to be done to make RRI an even better place to work. There's always a better way.

Best Regards,
Walt and Joe

Part III Highlights
Points to Remember

HR Fundamentals
Most fundamental of all HR issues is the philosophical foundation of how you really view your employees in the work environment you desire.

A Strategic Function
HR is just as important as all the other corporate functions, including sales and service, and should have an equal place of importance at the strategic planning table.

Diversity
In the global economy, workforce diversity (tolerance) is not an option—it's a must.

Age—Preference or Discrimination?
In today's workforce environment, where the demand for knowledge workers exceeds the supply, mandatory retirement ages are counterproductive.

Recruiting and Selecting
Know exactly what you're looking for, coupled with the most effective way to determine when you've found it. All the good and bad things in a company start here.

Mutual Expectations
Most relationship failures can be traced to lack of these up front.

Career Development
Successful companies view this as an investment, not a chore.

Evolution of Employee Quality
As companies grow, so too does the quality of employees, and some will invariably be left behind. Most can be retained productively.

Retention

The primary retention motivator is the culture itself. Looking forward to going to work each day with the people you like and the company you're proud of is the key to retention.

Pay and Benefits

Must reflect core values and culture.

Recognition Programs

A big part of motivation, but only if meaningful to all employees, who should play a major role in their design. Management builds in program sustainability.

Checking the Morale Pulse

You must find effective ways to regularly assess how well you're living up to your core values, culture, and the company side of mutual expectations.

PART IV

Leadership

FOLLOW ME

In the heat of battle the second lieutenant yells "Follow me!" as he charges the enemy emplacement. Will his troops follow, or sit where they are, or turn and run? The answer, of course, depends on the quality of the lieutenant's leadership skills over a period of time. All the training that the troops have received is for naught unless the organization (the squad, in this case) has the leadership to make it happen. Quite simply, any organization's effectiveness is as good (or bad) as the quality of its leadership.

Now that we've addressed the critical elements involved in building the foundation of fundamental beliefs and how they relate to all of those things required to recruit, develop, and retain the very best human talent, it's time to talk about the one indispensable ingredient absolutely required to maximize that human talent: leadership.

In previous sections of the book I've written about developing the philosophical foundation on which to build a business enterprise and how this is so instrumental in recruiting, developing, and retaining high-quality human talent.

However, all this good stuff is for naught unless the organization has the leadership to make it happen. Quite simply, any organization's future is as good (or bad) as the quality of its leadership.

Here are some interesting definitions from the *American Heritage Dictionary:*

> **Lead** (v). To show the way by going in advance.
>
> **Leader** (n). One who leads or guides.
>
> **Leadership** (n). The capacity or ability to lead.

There have been a number of milestones along my path to appreciating what leadership is all about.

When I was in the military, it was a given that officers always ate last. You always took care of your men before you took care of yourself. I'll never forget when I first reported for duty to the major who was my first military boss. He said to me, "Lieutenant, I'm sure you've heard the acronym RHIP (rank has its privileges), so I want you to be real clear as to my interpretation. First comes RHIR—rank has its responsibilities—which must be satisfied before you even start to think about RHIP."

Another milestone along the way was learning the hard way by experience in my first business. As our real estate company grew, a number of top-producing salesmen obviously rose to the top of the earnings column. Our reward was to make them office managers. What a horrendous mistake. The very personality dynamics that made them great salesmen were the antithesis of what was required to be great managers. So we ended up losing both good salesmen and lousy managers, a real lose/lose situation. We learned the hard way that the qualifications of managers (who should possess at least rudimentary leadership qualities) were very specific and distinct.

The next major milestone in my education was in my second business, The Hall Institute of Real Estate, which became the premier, national real estate training organization in the late sixties and throughout the seventies. In our early stages, we spent considerable time, money, and effort developing real estate agent training programs that had national application, and we were quite successful in having a large number of leading real estate firms throughout the country adopt these training programs.

After several years of marketing our agent training programs, we started to get feedback that although the programs were perceived as first rate, many real estate firms were having difficulty implementing the concepts and techniques contained in these training programs. It didn't take us long to find out who the culprit was. Guess what? Ineffective management. In other words, agents worked for ineffective office managers who were responsible for implementing, conducting, and following through with the principles and practices contained in the training program.

So, at that point, we shifted all our emphasis to researching, developing, and implementing a true management development program that went on to become the standard in the real estate industry. Lesson learned? Any program is only as good as the management responsible for implementing it.

At RRI I applied all the lessons I learned in my two previous businesses, particularly those lessons regarding leadership. Before sharing with you what I consider the most important leadership lessons learned during my twenty-five–year stint building RRI, let me first address the following question.

LEADERS—BORN, MADE, OR BOTH?

I believe leaders can be made, provided they were born with the requisite personality dynamics which, say behavioral scientists, are formed at a very early age.

For leaders, I believe key personality dynamics include moderate ego drive (the need to convince others), a high level of self-esteem and confidence, and strong empathy (the ability to sense and relate to the reactions of others).

With these innate attributes, potential leaders with the right personality dynamics can be made if they are given the right opportunities and experiences, and are in the right business environment. Uppermost in the experience category is crisis management.

There is another dimension to the question of born or made that is somewhat different than inherent personality dynamics and an encouraging environment. In the eighties and nineties, it was common to describe people who were very comfortable with themselves by saying they had their "act together." Looking back on those management failures I've experienced over the years, there were a number that make me think someone really didn't have their act together.

Abraham Maslow's *Hierarchy of Needs* always comes to mind when I hear an expression like that. Maslow came to believe that human beings are motivated by unsatisfied needs and that certain lower-level needs must be satisfied before higher-level needs can be addressed. As one need is satisfied, another pops up to take its place. The ultimate, fifth step he called "self-actualization," the act of unselfishly being or becoming all one is capable of. But preceding that ultimate plateau, one has to satisfy four lesser needs in this order: 1) Physiological needs (such as food, sleep, clothing, and shelter); 2) the need for safety and security; 3) the need for love and belonging; 4) the need for self-esteem.

The point here is that if energy is being consumed by the manager struggling to fulfill the need for love and belonging, or even self-esteem, there will be precious little energy left to lead others.

As I've said time and time again, all the good and bad things that can happen to an organization start with the recruiting and selection process. This is particularly true in the selection of managers and leaders.

Effective selection of managers and leaders should take considerable time, but that investment of time will be very well spent, because it is only over time that one can observe various candidates' basic personality dynamics and determine if, in fact, they have their acts together.

I really like this definition of leadership from the book *Leaders* by Warren Bennis and Burt Nanus: "The leaders have a positive self-regard called 'emotional wisdom'. This is characterized by an ability to accept people as they are; a capacity to approach things only in terms of the present; an ability to treat everyone, even close contacts, with courteous attention; an ability to trust others even when this seems risky; and an ability to do without constant approval and recognition."

LEADERSHIP LESSONS LEARNED

A Really Big Lesson for me occurred in the nineties and early years of the twenty-first century when I came to appreciate that the real test of leadership is not growth and profit in the short term but how consistently it can be achieved over the long haul. The relentless speed, complexity, competitiveness, and constant changes in the global economy and modern world demand that leadership be "super adaptive." It must be able to continually evolve the organization over an extended period of time under rapidly changing market conditions. So, don't judge the quality and staying power of any business over the short term; it's the long term that really counts.

If you need any examples of what happens to companies that can't adapt/ evolve quickly all you have to remember is the failure, in the recent past, of major players in the automobile, airline, recorded music, pharmaceutical, and newspaper industries, to name just a few.

Successful leaders have a vision and represent values that attract the best human talent. Winners want to be associated with winners. So, put another way, one of the most important responsibilities of a leader is to manage the values of the organization.

With that in mind, what follows is a summary of what I consider the most important leadership lessons I've learned over the years—most important because they related most directly to the relationship between values and business success.

Take Care of Everyone Else First

Over the years at RRI, I evolved the following end-of-fiscal-year approach. First, because we were a very capital-intensive company requiring significant lines of credit (over $100 million), we always started with the pre-tax profit level we knew would satisfy our lenders. Next, in addition to any performance bonuses to which they were entitled, all employees received AMEX gift certificates of between $50 and $300 for every year of service. Next, all management received bonuses based on their personal performance and company profitability. Finally, if there was anything left over, dividends were paid to me and other stockholders. If you take care of your employees first, last, and always, they'll take care of your customers and, therefore, you and the stockholders.

Leaders should always take care of followers before they take care of themselves, and this philosophy should permeate everything that goes on in the organization. For example, if budget dollars would result in a choice of either a company-wide picnic or a night on the town for some special event for just the management team, there should be no doubt whatsoever which one to choose.

This philosophy is analogous to the great athletic teams where the coaches view their fundamental job as carrying buckets of water for their players so they get on with the job of winning the game.

Executive Compensation

Executive compensation at most Fortune 1000 companies is seriously out of control. Many executives are not compensated according to performance; they are paid handsomely despite lousy performance. I believe it was in the late seventies that an American CEO was first paid over $1 million a year. CEOs at or near the same level quickly noticed, and the dam burst. The flood has yet to subside.

In many cases, executives have the incentive to manage on a short-term basis, reflecting the mentality of the financial markets. I believe that executive compensation should be primarily based on consistent long-term growth, profit, and increased shareholder value.

Many of the boards of directors of Fortune 1000 companies are asleep at the wheel and will remain so as long as their members have interlocking, fraternal-type relationships made up of friends, colleagues, and directors of companies with whom they have ongoing business relationships.

What do I think is the best and fairest approach to executive compensation? The lesson "Take care of everyone else first" will give you a good idea of where I'm coming from.

First, I strongly believe that the top person in the organization, the CEO, should have a maximum base salary that is no more than seven to ten times the average salary paid to other employees. After all, what's the worth to the organization of the CEO, relative to the rest of the employee population? At RRI, seven times the average salary was the top of the pay range—that was me. Keep in mind that my salary capped all other executive/senior management base salaries.

Second, the overall growth and profitability of the company is the executive staff's primary responsibility. Senior management responsible for a specific company function or functions should receive a percentage of salary bonus (up to 10 percent) for achieving their own challenging performance objectives and another percentage of salary (say, another 10 percent) based on overall company profitability and margin performance.

As CEO, my personal performance component was based on achieving challenging, long-term organizational growth objectives that were set for the overall company.

Ultimately, all forms of compensation, at all levels of the organization, should be viewed by all employees as fair and equitable and in keeping with an enlightened culture and core values. I hope there will come a day when huge, unwarranted paydays for executives are viewed as shameful and those who milk their companies for every dime are scorned.

My thoughts on executive compensation are summarized much more powerfully and eloquently by Peter F. Drucker in his *Wall Street Journal* article of May 23, 1977 titled "Is Executive Pay Excessive?"

> If and when the attack on the 'excessive compensation of executives' is launched—and I very much fear that it will come soon—business will complain about the public's 'economic illiteracy' and will bemoan the public's 'hostility to business.' But business will have only itself to blame.

> It is a business responsibility, but also a business self-interest, to develop a sensible executive compensation structure that portrays economic reality and asserts and codifies the achievement of U.S. business in this century: the steady narrowing of the income gap between the 'boss man' and the 'working man'.

To say that he was prophetic is obviously an understatement. When the U.S. was primarily a manufacturing economy, there was a natural distance between the educated, knowledge-based boss man and the labor-oriented working man. Today, both boss man and working man are essentially "knowledge workers" existing in a global economy based on technology and information. There is no "natural distance" that warrants huge differences in compensation.

Charisma vs. Character

When it comes to leadership, beware the charmer. All too often, the publicity seeker's personality camouflages a lack of character and leadership interest. Give me a solid citizen with strength of character who is focused on meaningful, challenging, and achievable objectives; who puts his or her team first; and who can thrive on the team's achievements, not his or her own. In a June 22, 2004 *Wall Street Journal* editorial article commenting on the publication of Bill Clinton's memoirs, it stated: "We wish Mr. Clinton well with his book promotion. But we suspect the judgment of many readers will be the one that the late TV commentator Eric Sevareid once made, for very different reasons, about Harry Truman: 'It's character, just character.'"

Self-Confidence

The understanding between me and the people who directly reported to me was that they were expected to tell me, when it was warranted, that I was full of *&@! without any fear of reprisal. The deal was that I also had the same rights. No one was supposed to get whacked out of shape in the process. Our culture was very participatory and collaborative, starting from the top. Frank, open discussion of various pros and cons invariably led to the right decision for the company, whether or not that decision reflected my opinion or the opinions of individual members of the executive council.

A true mark of self-confidence is the ability to look forward to learning from failures and mistakes. The willingness of top management to let members of the management team—the company's leadership—make mistakes is, in my opinion, the mark of a great company. This attitude starts at the top. You might say to members of the management team, "I have a lot of faith in you, and I trust you to do a great job. In fact, I expect it. But I also expect you will make mistakes (as I have), and that's okay—as long as you learn from those mistakes. I'm here for any advice you feel you may need, but that request must come from you. I'm not going to be looking over your shoulder."

Self-Discipline

There is no leadership without self-discipline. When you have to or should do something you really don't want to do, self-discipline can be defined as the acceptance and willingness (albeit grudging willingness) to do what you don't want to do when you don't want to do it.

All leaders have acquired self-discipline their own unique way, and if you are interviewing a candidate for a management position it is incumbent on you to find out if they have it and how they got it.

I was well into adulthood when I came to appreciate that my self-discipline—getting in the habit of doing what I didn't want to do, when I didn't want to do it—was acquired without my conscious knowledge starting at about age six or seven. From that age until I left for college at age eighteen, I woke up to the rooster every morning and went out to do the chores—tend to the horses, cows, and chickens. I never really enjoyed it—but I did it. And thanks to my mother's encouragement and perseverance, I started taking piano lessons at age six and continued them until age eighteen. Again, there were many, many days I would have much preferred to be out playing ball with my buddies instead of sitting down to my piano practice.

The point is simple: when assessing leadership potential, always look for candidates' background and experience that verifies the ingrained habit of being able and willing to do what they don't want to do—when they don't want to do it.

Micromanaging vs. Macromanaging

If you've got the right horses, you had better macromanage and let 'em run. Give them the responsibility and corresponding authority all the way. If you don't have the managerial talent you're comfortable with, you are going to have to micromanage, which means getting involved and putting your stamp on every decision. When this happens, your company and its future become totally dependent on only you, which can be very limiting and eventually destructive in the long term.

I speak from firsthand experience. As I mentioned earlier, I had virtually no capital available when I started to build each of the three businesses I created, so I had to macro *and* micromanage out of necessity. As a consequence, I developed some truly bad habits that were difficult to break as we started to grow and needed to recruit competent managerial talent. Shortly after I commenced hiring this competent talent, some serious problems started to occur. In retrospect, all of these problems were traceable to me and my ingrained habit of sticking my nose in everyone else's operation.

I'm particularly indebted to one such manager who, after several months on the job, came to me with his letter of resignation. It took me completely by surprise, as I thought he was doing a great job and we were getting along well together. When I asked him why, here's what he said: "Walt, let me give you an analogy: say I'm a gifted landscape painter and you've hired me to paint you a masterpiece. So I set up my easel, lay out my paints, brushes and other supplies, and start to do just that. Not long after I start, I feel you looking over my shoulder, offering suggestions like 'I think you should tone down that color,' or 'that tree seems a little out of place.' My masterpiece for you is no longer mine, so I'm breaking down my easel, packing up my paints and brushes, and I'm out of here."

I listened, took it to heart, thanked him for his candor, and asked him to give me a day or two to reflect on his comments before we formalized a parting of the ways. Two days later I told him that I had really thought about what he told me and had to tell him that I agreed with his assessment that I wasn't letting him do the job for which he was hired and was very capable of performing.

I bit the bullet and never looked back. He stayed with the company and we worked together for over twenty-five years. That bad habit taught me an important lesson.

No commentary on delegation of authority is complete without at least a few comments on the potential for abdication of responsibility, so let me quote from the master, Peter F. Drucker, in his *Wall Street Journal* article of March 24, 1987 titled "Management Lessons of Irangate":

> In one of the most common but also most unforgivable management mistakes—the Reagan administration confused delegation of authority with abdication of responsibility. A chief executive officer must delegate. Otherwise, he'll end up like Gulliver in Lilliput, ineffectual and ensnared in details, as were Lyndon Johnson and Jimmy Carter.

> But delegation requires greater accountability and tighter control. Delegation requires clear assignment of a specific task, clear definition of the expected results and a deadline. Above all it requires that the subordinate to whom a task is delegated keep the boss fully informed. It is the subordinate's job to alert the boss immediately to any possible 'surprise'—rather than to try to 'protect' the boss against surprises, as Mr. Reagan's subordinates apparently did. If they keep

surprises away from the boss, they invariably will end up making him look incompetent or not in control or a liar—or all three.

Consistency and Trust

The best leaders and managers are those who are very even keeled, consistent people their teams view as solid and steady. Show me a neurotic manager, and I'll show you a neurotic team with big swings in the results category. The best leaders and managers are trusted. Their word is their bond. It all boils down to respect, not love. An expression I once heard went something like this: if a manager can't exist on the respect of his or her team (as opposed to love and affection), that manager is doomed to mediocrity. Respect flows to the leader who is consistent and trustworthy, who lives the company's core values, and who always puts the interests of his or her team first.

On Decisions

Leadership, of course, means making decisions—all kinds of decisions. All day, every day. Many minor, and a few with major strategic implications.

In my business experience it took me a long time to appreciate that, regarding decisions, *the moment of absolute certainty never arrives.* There are always the proverbial "what-ifs" and the high probability of unintended consequences. So, starting with that premise, let me share with you what I feel are the two keys to consistently making major decisions that will have the most positive impact on long-term growth and profit: core values and consensus.

Core Values

Assuming a morally sound, ethical, and practical set of core values is fully embedded in your culture, they will give you the philosophical base to make and define the right decisions and, most importantly, the "why" behind those decisions. If the decision is compatible with your core values it has the highest chance of being regarded, inside and outside the organization, as the right decision. Conversely, if it's not compatible, the odds are almost 100 percent that sooner or later it will be a failure, and viewed as such by everyone affected.

Consensus

Major decisions affect many people: employees, management, customers, major suppliers, creditors, families, and more. Once the need to make that big decision became clear, the very first thing our executive council did was to clearly define who, exactly, was going to be impacted by that decision.

If it was a decision about any aspect of operations, we always got employee representatives from the groups affected to work with us in the decision-making process, based on the principle that people support what they help create. Also, there can be a perception disconnect between management and the employees who are actually carrying out the work. Not being on the firing line every day, management doesn't experience the day-to-day reality of the actual work involved in the decision. We learned that if the employees who would ultimately implement the decision had been exposed to all the considerations (pro and con) up front, the decision would be implemented effectively, with no loss of productivity.

A synonym for implementation is "execution," and much has been written about this subject. However, in my estimation it doesn't take a whole book on the subject to describe what is really quite simple, based on good old common sense.

Assuming the decision was a good one—based on your core values and participation of all the affected players in the decision-making process—our implementation (or "execution") protocols can be summarized as follows:

The Plan

The same people who were involved in the decision-making process should put together the implementation plan—and communicate it to their various constituencies within the company.

Like any good plan it should have:

- ❖ A stated objective (what, precisely, is to be accomplished?)
- ❖ A completion date (by when?)
- ❖ Benchmarks (if required—with interim target dates)
- ❖ Accountability (who is responsible for what?)
- ❖ Measurements (how are we going to measure achievement of incremental steps/stages and overall objectives?)
- ❖ Monitoring (who is going to document performance of objectives and how are they going to do it?)

Trust

Trust is mutual. If leaders give it, followers will reciprocate. But trust can be lost quickly, and once it's lost, it takes a long time to win back.

A company's fundamental beliefs—its core values, culture, mutual expectations, and leadership expectations—should set the foundation and tone for mutual trust throughout the organization. At RRI, in our official literature on culture, we said:

Informality and Trust

We don't stand on ceremony, formality, or bureaucracy. Rather, we believe a relaxed, informal atmosphere, based on mutual trust, provides the best environment for continued growth and success.

Candid Communication

When communicating with our employees, clients, and preferred service partners, we always attempt to 'tell it the way it is' in a candid, straightforward manner.

From *Mutual Expectations (page 67-69)*
(*What employees can expect from RRI*)
> Honesty in advising about corporate
> objectives and the current and projected
> economic viability of the company.

Honesty and trust go together. You can't have one without the other. The company's core values, culture, and other guiding principles clearly set the overall tone and framework for the company's leadership to extend trust to their followers. It will be paid back many times over.

However, one word of caution: trust, but verify. Statistically, no matter how good your selection process and your organizational principles are, a small percentage of employees—many in positions of financial responsibility and accountability—may have a larcenous streak that you do not want to encourage by lack of independent verification.

In my entire business career, only once did I trust completely and not verify, a decision that ultimately cost me and other employee stockholders a considerable amount of money. Had I set up an independent verification of the funds flowing into and out of our organization, this would not have occurred.

If and when something like this happens in your organization, the only advice I have is that you not allow an isolated, negative situation of this nature, no matter how monetarily significant, to contaminate and change all the positive things that are good and valuable in your culture—including the principle of mutual trust. Just chalk the bad apple up to a truly serious, but nonetheless valuable, mistake from which you can really learn. Life goes on, so get on with it.

Firing

No matter how effective your recruiting and selection process is, every leader is confronted with the need to sever a business relationship, and it is never easy. Ideally, involuntary separation should not come as a total surprise to the affected employee. If ongoing critical discussions regarding negative performance are shared with the employee and documented in the form of coaching sessions and negative performance reviews, an employee will always be aware of his or her standing within the organization. Strategically, every organization should strive to set specific, measurable performance expectations and objectives and monitor them on a regular basis.

In this litigious day and age, it is imperative to clearly document the supporting reasons leading up to an employee's termination. Each integral component of documentation must cohesively align and substantiate the clearly stated company policies and practices regarding performance expectations and objectives. This will avoid costly, time-consuming litigation and promote a strong sense of understanding of the professional practices required by the organization.

Once the decision is made to fire someone, and you are comfortable that you have the necessary documentation to warrant the action, don't wait—get to it and do it face-to-face. Offer as much post-job assistance and advice as you feel is appropriate. A genuine concern for your employee's post-employment welfare can go a long way to making this a less unpleasant experience for both you and the employee.

Finally, regardless of whether or not you think there is any possibility that the employee may be alleging any kind of wrongful discharge rationale, it is a good practice to always have a witness attend your severance meetings. If you have an HR department, it should obviously be an HR representative. If you don't, get another member of the management staff to attend.

The Importance of Exercise

An effective leader feels good and has a high energy level throughout the day.

Both my father and grandfather were great athletes. My Dad used to say, "When you least feel like it, that's the time when exercise will do you the most good." And I found out the hard way that he was absolutely right.

When I was building my second business, I was literally on the road—and "on"—all the time, from getting ready for my departure flight to waiting in the baggage area upon return. I was in my late thirties and early forties at the time and I was becoming severely run down, with lower and lower energy levels. After several years of this I was on a return flight one day and feeling especially lousy when my Dad's philosophy came to me. Exercise was the furthest thing from my mind at the time, but I said to myself, "What the heck, I'll go right to the gym after landing and give it a go." The rest, as they say, is history. I arrived home a new man—energized, happy, and feeling top-notch both physically and mentally.

From that day on I made the commitment to myself that I would exercise at least five days a week. I would pencil exercise into my schedule as an appointment with myself, and consider it just as important as any business appointment. To this day I work up a good sweat, get the heart pumping, and lift some weights. I feel great.

I carried this philosophy over to my businesses. All officers and directors were provided with health club memberships, provided they used them at least three days a week. Generally, we promoted the personal benefits of exercise (and diet) throughout the company in every way we could, without being preachy or intrusive.

Over the course of time, it became quite obvious to me that the staff members who exercised regularly were far more productive (particularly in the afternoon) and more likely to exceed their performance objective.

LEADERSHIP IN TURBULENT TIMES

The inevitable expansion and contraction of our global economy will present challenges along the way. Periods of economic growth will necessitate increases in staffing, salary, and benefits in order to remain competitive, while on the down side, staff reductions and/or reduction of benefits, all too often result in losing irreplaceable talent forever.

Be that as it may, my philosophy on the subject can be summed up by one of my father's favorite business axioms: "In the good times prepare for the bad times – and in the bad times prepare for the good times." However, I do appreciate that it's tough to think positively in negative times, and negatively in positive times.

You might well think: nice to say – tough to do. Not if your organization has a set of fundamental beliefs that are practical, ethical, employee-centered and equally client-centric, as previously described in Part II.

When tough economic times hit it usually results in management intensively focusing on reducing head count and cutting every cost possible – to the exclusion of everything else, like the need to retain the talent they will need when the market turns. Having lived through and survived a number of recessions during my business career (three of them major) here are the lessons learned:

Avoid "Knee Jerk" Response

Think it out carefully. Develop a cost-reduction plan and approach after getting input from all management staff and a broad representation of employees.

Communicate (Frequently and Honestly)

Employees are looking for the unvarnished truth – not surprises. These are emotional times for all concerned, making it very challenging to keep employees engaged and focused during cost-cutting efforts. This calls for hands on, consistent, candid, caring, coordinated communication from the management staff, from the CEO on down the line.

Share the Pain

When employees are asked to sacrifice with extra work load or reduction in pay and/or work week, it is a must that management make a proportionate sacrifice. Walk the talk.

Get Employees Involved

Think of ways to keep the employees you want to retain involved in what they can control, such as recognition/rewards for improving customer satisfaction and submitting workable ideas for cutting cost and/or increasing revenue. These employees should feel they are part of the solution – not part of the problem.

Rethink Sales/Profit Targets and Production Objectives

Make sure they fit the reality of a reduced market opportunity and work effort required.

Be Careful of Across-the-Board Layoffs

A reduction of work week/pay for all employees may be a first step (and hopefully the only one), but if that doesn't do the trick, out of necessity you may need to reduce administrative/support staff more than those engaged in sales and service or production.

There Is An Upside

Smart management sees downturns as also having some upside as well. New talent that needs to be brought in is generally less costly; and there often is the potential to gain market share if competitors cut back more than they needed to. However, the biggest potential upside is the lasting benefit of effective, demonstrated crisis management. Employees (and investors and creditors) never forget the company that weathered the bad times and came out in one piece with the talent they wanted and needed. That's Leadership with a capital "L."

LEADERSHIP ISSUES

Over the years we developed a set of "leadership issues" to provide a frame of reference for our leadership team. These issues were used for developing and prioritizing leadership meetings or agenda subjects for discussion.

Typically, prior to any kind of meeting involving the management staff, our president/COO would e-mail the entire management staff and poll them as to which three leadership issues they felt were presently most important to discuss. Invariably the majority of the management staff picked the same three, which then found their way onto the agenda.

We came to the conclusion that many of these issues were just as appropriate for discussion with all employees in any number of venues, such as company meetings, our *RRI Insider* intranet news, or at individual office town meetings.

Here are the issues we came up with over time. I'm sorry that I can't remember the person who drafted the original set of issues that we refined and built upon, because I would like to give that person credit.

Management: What does it mean to be a manager? What are the roles and capabilities that distinguish "managers" from others in the organization?

Leadership: What is the distinction between management and leadership? What does it take to lead? Are leaders born or made? Can everyone aspire to be a leader?

Clients: What do clients really want? What are the foundations of client loyalty? What does it mean to be client-centered? How can a company consistently exceed client expectations?

Global: What does it mean to be global? Must a company be global? How does one build cohesion in global enterprises? When should one respect local differences? When should one ignore local differences?

The Future: How will our world be different in the future? How is the context of leadership and management changing? Can we accurately predict the future? Can we prepare for it?

Renewal: What are the secrets of continued organizational vitality? Why do some companies thrive on change, while others are destroyed by change? Is it possible to redirect the energies of a company?

Competition: How does one create a sustainable, competitive advantage? What are the strategies for winning in a highly competitive marketplace? How does one capture a disproportionate share of profits in an industry or industry segment?

Efficiency: How can we do more with less? How can we maximize the ratio of output over input? How can we become the world's most profitable service provider?

Strategy: Where are we heading? What is our destiny? What is it that unites us? What are we trying to build? Where and how can we win?

LEADERSHIP EXPECTATIONS

In Part II, I shared with you the idea of mutual expectations between the company and its employees. The logical extension of these *Mutual Expectations* is what we developed as *Leadership Expectations*, which are reproduced below. Once again, it's important to point out that the development of these

Leadership Expectations was a company-wide, all-employee effort over an extended period of time. Everyone had a chance to give his/her own input as to what the company should expect from its leadership team.

This became another fundamental belief of the company designed to integrate and be compatible with our vision, core values, culture, and mutual expectations.

Leadership Expectations

At RRI, employees in leadership (management) positions are responsible for and are empowered to manage functions that are critical to the company's growth and success.

The RRI Leadership Team is expected to:

- ❖ Ensure that both the company and the employees they lead meet RRI's *Mutual Expectations;*
- ❖ Manage by example, setting a positive image for others;
- ❖ Represent and act in the best interests of the company, its employees, and its clients;
- ❖ Exemplify a positive 'can do' attitude at all times;
- ❖ Set the highest standards for work quality, professional appearance, and demeanor;
- ❖ Listen to the team, and let them know their input counts even when suggestions can't be implemented;
- ❖ Make sure the team appreciates how their work impacts other areas of the company;
- ❖ Promote communication and positive interaction with other company departments;
- ❖ Provide relevant feedback to motivate the team and provide opportunities for further personal growth and development;
- ❖ Keep the team informed of team and company initiatives and developments;

❖ Clearly articulate RRI's core values/culture and department ground rules;

❖ Justify the benefits to be derived from all costs and expenses incurred in their business unit; and

❖ Spread work evenly, ensuring that everyone on the team is consistently challenged and productive.

Because the philosophy *promote from within* was our ideal approach to advancement (although not always possible, particularly for the highest level jobs), we worked hard to recognize managerial talent at all times.

Generally, this talent was recognized by the existing management team, who observed how a potential candidate interrelated with team members and those outside the team at all levels. Because of our interrelated fundamental beliefs, management had a very good idea of what we were looking for in our managers. Particularly applicable was our *Leadership Expectations*; that is, the document was helpful to both the hiring manager and the candidate manager, giving both a good frame of reference.

If we—or the job applicant—had any doubt about the arrangement, we usually used the title "manager candidate" for some predetermined period of time, so that the individual candidate could save face if the position wasn't a good fit.

MEASURING RESULTS

Anything worth doing is worth doing well, and it's important to measure results. Described below is our leadership assessment survey, which over time proved to be an invaluable tool in the ongoing development of our leadership team.

The results of each manager's survey were incorporated into his or her overall semi-annual performance review. It was made quite clear that the objective of the leadership assessment survey was to improve leadership skills and results, not to criticize leadership styles.

To: All RRI Employees
From: Human Resources
Date: October 21, 2002
Subject: Management Assessment 2002

To further enhance our company-wide communication initiatives we have developed the attached management assessment online document [see page 118].

Please click on the customized link below, which will provide you access to both the introduction and assessment document. **As a result of this link, you will be able to complete the requested information both anonymously and confidentially.** We hope that you will be able to complete and return the assessment to HR no later than Friday, October 25.

Based on our *Leadership Expectations,* we have incorporated these principles into the evaluation tool. Clearly, the success of our leadership team is vital to ensure our company's ongoing growth and success. Keeping this in mind, in order for the management team's performance review process to begin, we would ask that you take some time to complete this confidential document assessing your specific manager by using the button below.

As you know from the past year, IT created this online capability for the evaluation process which will ease your ability to complete this critical document in an anonymous and confidential manner. We hope this procedure will ensure the high rate of return necessary to measure and evaluate our leadership's effectiveness.

Any questions relative to this review process may be directed to any member of the human resources team.

THANK YOU!

Human Resources

Management Assessment

Please select your manager's name: | - - SELECT ONE - - ▼ |

Leadership Expectations

At RRI, employees in leadership (management) positions are responsible for and are empowered to manage functions that are critical to the company's continued growth and success. In light of this, please rate your manager on each Expectation based on the following scale:

     ① – Ineffective

     ② – Somewhat Effective

     ③ – Effective

     ④ – Mostly Effective

     ⑤ – Always Effective

The RRI Leadership Team is Expected To:

① ② ③ ④ ⑤	Ensure that both the company and the employees they lead meet RRI's *Mutual Expectations*
① ② ③ ④ ⑤	Manage by example, setting a positive image for others
① ② ③ ④ ⑤	Represent and act in the best interests of the company, its employees, and its clients
① ② ③ ④ ⑤	Always exemplify a positive "can do" attitude
① ② ③ ④ ⑤	Set the highest standards for work quality, professional appearance, and demeanor
① ② ③ ④ ⑤	Listen to the team and let them know their input counts, even though suggestions can't always be implemented
① ② ③ ④ ⑤	Make sure the team appreciates how their work impacts other areas of the company

① ② ③ ④ ⑤	Promote communication and positive interaction with other company departments
① ② ③ ④ ⑤	Provide relevant feedback to motivate the team and provide opportunities for further personal growth and development
① ② ③ ④ ⑤	Keep their team informed of team and company initiatives and developments. Clearly articulate the company core values and department ground rules
① ② ③ ④ ⑤	Spread work evenly, ensuring that everyone on the team is consistently challenged and productive

Describe your manager's strengths as you see and experience them:

Describe your manager's developmental needs (i.e., skills, behavior) as you see and experience them:

PART IV HIGHLIGHTS
POINTS TO REMEMBER

LEADERS

Born, made, or both? Leaders can be made if born with the requisite personality dynamics and have the right opportunities to test and apply their leadership skills.

TAKE CARE OF EVERYONE ELSE FIRST

If you take care of your employees first, last, and always, they'll take care of your clients and customers and, therefore, the owners.

EXECUTIVE COMPENSATION

In the U.S., executive compensation is out of control. It's non-performance based. CEOs should have a base salary that is no more than seven to ten times the average employee salary.

CHARISMA VS. CHARACTER

Beware the charmer and publicity lover. All too often it's a camouflage for lack of character and/or leadership interest and capability.

SELF-CONFIDENCE

The most effective CEOs tell those that report directly to them to tell them they are full of *&@! when it's warranted, as long as the CEOs can reciprocate.

MICROMANAGING VS. MACROMANAGING

If you've got the right horses, let 'em run with accountable responsibility and authority.

CONSISTENCY AND TRUST

The best leaders are even keeled, very consistent, and very trusted. Their word is their bond. It boils down to respect, not love.

TRUST

Trust is mutual. If leaders give it, followers will reciprocate. Trust once lost takes a long time to win back. In financial positions, trust, but always verify.

FIRING

Termination should not come as a surprise. Offer as much post-job assistance and/or advice as you feel appropriate. Genuine concern can make this a less unpleasant experience for both parties.

ABOUT EXERCISE

The leader who consistently feels good throughout the day and has a high energy level is effective. Exercise regularly.

LEADERSHIP ISSUES

An established set of leadership issues can really help develop and prioritize management meeting and discussion agendas.

LEADERSHIP EXPECTATIONS

Every employee in any kind of a management position should have a crystal-clear understanding of what is expected regarding leadership. Management has to find ways to make sure these expectations are being met from the employees' point of view.

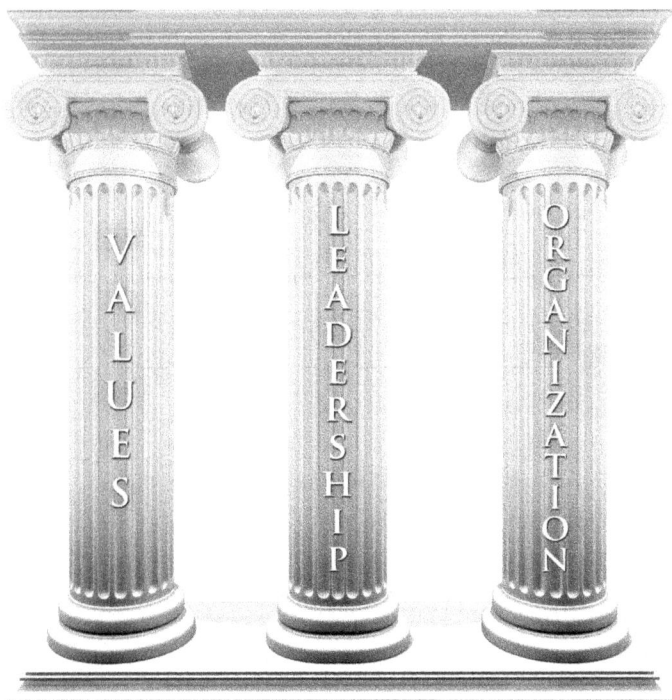

PART V

Organization

IMPACT OF ORGANIZATIONAL STRUCTURE ON CLIENTS

Your firm is a client of a financial services company and you're the firm's major contact point for this company. One day you receive a monthly report and invoice that are totally erroneous, so you immediately call your contact, from whom you purchased the services. His response is, "IT and the finance group are all screwed up, and I'll get right on them." You know this company is tightly organized by function; the sales group with whom you've worked is viewed separately from the other sectors, including IT and finance.

If this company was organized around *process*, instead of function, chances are the response would have been more like this: "Gee, I'm really sorry; looks like we fouled up. I'll get together with my colleagues in IT and finance and we'll get it squared away pronto." The "we're all in this together for you" approach is obviously much more pleasing to the client.

This is where you put it all together—the structure you feel is best suited to aid you in fulfilling your mission and achieving your vision on a long-term basis.

As I said in Part III, the only sustainable competitive advantage any business can achieve in the future is the quality of the human talent it can recruit, develop and retain - people with knowledge that continues to grow and keep the organization ahead of the competition. Your major assets are human talent and knowledge. A company's core values, culture, mutual expectations, and leadership expectations should all evolve around these fundamental considerations. It follows that your organizational structure should do likewise.

FUNCTION VS. PROCESS

For years, the traditional organizational structure was built around different departments and their functions, i.e., marketing, finance, sales, service, human resources, purchasing, legal, and others. One of the key assumptions underlying this form of structure was that the business process would remain constant, with minor or very little change. "Traditionally structured organizations were inherently designed to maintain the status quo rather than to respond to the changing demands of the market." (Melvin Anshen, *Harvard Business Review*). However, in today's business world, the work that needs to be done is changing constantly.

Traditionally, functional structures tended to be vertical within an organization. That is, the knowledge and skill each functional unit possessed stayed pretty much within that functional unit. Conversely, in a participatory, collaborative culture, horizontal units interrelate and together do the work of the organization.

Organizational structures with vertical walls based on functions have proven to support and perpetuate top-heavy hierarchies; they are very ineffective and expensive in terms of both human and financial capital.

In the simplest terms, most companies' major functions and processes evolve around marketing/sales and service. One creates and sells the product or service, i.e., makes the promise, and the other delivers on that promise, i.e. provides the service or product.

Typically, in the old, traditional functional structure, there were the usual support functions like finance, human resources, administration, purchasing, legal, and IT. Many times, the service component itself had a number of sub-functions.

However, it has become quite apparent to today's successful businesses that the old days of the major sales/service line functions supported by a number of staff functions are obsolete. One way or another, every person in the organization is inexorably tied to marketing/sales and service, and getting the work of the organization done: creating, selling, and servicing.

At RRI, it became exceedingly clear in the early stages that a late, erroneous invoice issued by finance—or an incorrect report produced by IT—was just as detrimental to sales and service as anything employees within these functions could do. Conversely, if billing and reports were timely and accurate, it was an enhancement of sales and service. It's not function that's critical, it's process.

Let me give you an example. At RRI, our organizational structure was built on the work needing to be done. We had a large number of employees involved in the end of our typical cycle, which was client billing. The beginning of the cycle started with client initiation; the corporate client would contact us and advise of a newly relocated employee. Our service cycle with that one transferee and family would typically last 120 days.

Our volume of activity was highly unpredictable, changing constantly. If we had been structured by function, think for a moment what would happen if all of a sudden initiations went through the roof, and our relocation counselors on the service team couldn't handle the volume. We would have had no choice but to try adding new counselors or turning down the business (unthinkable). However, because we were structured on process and believed in cross-training, we were able to pull certain selected and specially trained billers from the end of the cycle and move them to the front of the cycle until things leveled off. The result was that our clients were happy, with no need for knee-jerk, expensive recruiting of new employees.

So the key is to organize around process, not function, and in so doing flatten the hierarchy. The concept is to structure the organization based on a field of work needing to be done, versus a structure built around jobs.

In a December, 1994 *Fortune* article by William Bridges titled "The End of the Job", he said, "De-jobbed companies share at least four traits: 1) they encourage rank and file employees to make the kind of operating decisions that used to be reserved for managers; 2) they give people the information that they need to make such decisions—information that used to be given only to managers; 3) they give employees lots of training to create the kind of understanding of business and financial issues that no one but an owner or an executive used to be concerned with; and 4) they give people a stake in the fruits of their labor—a share of company profits." This was a perfect description of the type of organization we created at RRI.

THE ELLIPTICAL ORGANIZATION

At RRI we created what we called an *elliptical* organizational structure. This structure is reproduced on page 133.

Note that we were organized around what we acknowledged was the center of our business universe, which, in turn, created an organization without boundaries dedicated to doing what had to be done to satisfy the needs and expectations of our clients and transferees.

CORE PROCESSES/COMPETENCIES

Today, it is almost universally accepted in the business community that to become and remain successful, a company should 1) clearly understand its core processes, i.e., how it makes money; 2) make sure the company's core competencies mirror these core processes; and 3) outsource to qualified suppliers all other functions or jobs that are not core processes.

As management guru Peter F. Drucker said: "Outsourcing is a necessity. Outsourcing is not so much about cost cutting ('illusory') as it is about improving the quality of work that others can do better than you. You should outsource everything for which there is no career track that can lead to senior management."

Core processes and competencies are directly related to KFSs (key factors for success), the realization by the company's leadership that there are, at best, only a few critical and strategically significant functions/processes and related competencies that will account for continued success.

At RRI our core processes related specifically to getting and keeping corporate clients, which we reflected in our *Performance Standards,* as described in Part III.

Our related core competencies were described as follows:

Client Consulting

Working with clients to develop the best total solution to their unique employee relocation needs.

Transferee Counseling

Working with transferees to make their relocation as pleasant and stress-free as possible.

Teamwork Building

Building effective relationships with clients, their relocating employees, and our preferred service partners.

BUSINESS PROCESS OUTSOURCING (BPO)

As we gradually outsourced every function that was not a part of our core processes, we learned some valuable lessons. First, make absolutely sure to describe and explain in great detail the functions and activities you are intending to outsource. Second, search the market and, hopefully, invite a minimum of three qualified suppliers to bid on your business.

Next, I would recommend that you invite all three in so you can respond to questions they may have about your request for proposal (RFP). This will also give you the opportunity for a preliminary observation of the culture and values of each candidate.

After each candidate submits its response to your RFP (assuming they are all in the ballpark regarding price), invite them all back to present their responses in person and answer all your questions. At both the first and return visit, it is imperative that you have in attendance the management and representative employees from the functional groups who would be working directly with the supplier.

The company-to-company cultural fit and the fit between the operational groups of both companies are absolutely critical. Even if the price is higher with the one you all feel is the best candidate, and you can't get them to reduce their price, it's best to choose the one you're most comfortable with unless the cost differential between the first and second choice is substantial. Overall, we attached 70 percent value to capabilities and the mutual comfort zone, 30 percent to price.

In the purchasing department of the Royal Bank of Canada, there is a wall plaque that states, "The sweetness of a low price is forgotten long after the bitterness of poor service."

Some Lessons Learned

Long before we learned enough to establish the BPO approach, our first attempt at outsourcing a major function was an unmitigated disaster.

We knew that in order to stay competitive, we had to migrate away from our legacy mainframe system to a wide area network with a Web-based interface for client and service provider access.

At the time we made the decision, we had no one on staff who was totally conversant with this technology, so after checking a few references (provided for us by the supplier) we went with the first outsourcing organization that sounded good to us. To make a very long, painful, and expensive story short, we got lousy service and ultimately were held hostage by their threat to shut us down if we didn't accede to their demands to continue retaining them.

After accruing some substantial legal and accounting fees, we were able to extricate ourselves from this outfit, and here's the main lesson we learned: in addition to normal screening (checking references, history, and credit), make absolutely sure to have someone you trust and who has knowledge about the technology interview and assess the technical competency of the supplier.

Right after this fiasco, we decided to build our own internal IT department. The very first thing I did was to interview the very experienced IT directors of our law and accounting firms. I asked them to serve as our primary evaluators of the technical expertise of the candidates we were considering.

As described earlier, we were very good at determining if there was a cultural comfort zone with various candidates. However, if you don't have someone on staff who has the expertise to also judge the technical competency of the applicant, you had better find someone you trust on the outside who does.

Our IT venture was our only failed outsourcing effort. We learned enough from that experience to avoid anything resembling it thereafter. Another valuable lesson we learned was that once the relationship was established, you had to communicate and manage that relationship with the outsourced supplier just as you would an internal unit. In essence, we treated them as family, and the results were outstanding. We put it this way: "We are committed to building a long-lasting partnership with each of our clients. Partnering also means respecting our preferred service partners and their role as an integral part of the RRI service delivery team." And, in our *Mutual Expectations* handbook, we added that we expected all RRI employees to "treat RRI's service partners and each other with dignity and respect, regardless of work performed or job level."

MIGRATING THE BUSINESS MODEL

As businesses grow and prosper, effective leadership will inevitably see opportunities to add additional services for their established customer base and/or try to create an additional new client base.

A macro example would be General Motors and General Motors Acceptance Corporation (GMAC), its finance company subsidiary. At a certain point in GM's growth, it saw the need and opportunity to directly extend credit to the buyers of its automobiles, as opposed to the previous practice of its customers obtaining financing from a bank or finance company. GMAC became more profitable than all of GM's automotive operations combined.

My first business (real estate) and last (global relocation services) offer some "micro" examples. In my real estate business, we first concentrated on one thing—providing real estate services to sellers and buyers of homes. Once that was fairly well established, we formed a mortgage company and then an insurance company. In other words, we migrated from a business model of one company providing one service to a new holding company which owned three companies providing three distinct services to the same consumers—sellers and buyers of homes.

There were several particularly important lessons we learned in those early years. First, it was key that we concentrated on one thing. That one thing was aimed at a retail (one-at-a-time) marketplace. In Part I, I wrote about the key factors of success (KFS) and the wisdom of concentrating major resources in the early stages of the company on a single, strategically significant function. In other words, don't migrate sideways or upwards until your KFS and company are well established. Also, don't jump markets without considerable thought and planning. By this I mean jumping from retail to wholesale marketing or vice versa—I liken this to the difference between poker and bridge. The cards are the same (people are people) but the games and timing are very different.

Not too long after our three real estate–related companies were really humming, I had the bright idea that if we developed a portfolio of six different home plans and specifications reflecting our reading of market demand, coupled with the development of a stable of builders and land developers who all agreed to a specific price for each home above the land, we would have a real winner.

We quickly found out that our whole approach to marketing and sales was very different in this case. We were selling one person, the builder or land developer, as a conduit to sell to a multitude of home buyers. In that regard, it became what we called a wholesale marketing situation, which required a whole different set of personnel, systems, and mission, and which had to be truly divorced from our retail operations in everything but ownership. Accordingly, we formed a new company called Associated Builders' Group. As soon as we made it totally autonomous, it became highly successful. It needed to be autonomous because its target market was quite different from our other customers. Making this distinction made all the difference in the world.

During the twenty-five year lifetime of RRI, we evolved our business model from one company providing one service (helping corporate clients relocate their employees) to a number of companies providing a wide variety of services to the corporate marketplace, including such things as consulting services

(The Relocation Institute, Inc.), real estate closing services (Relocation Closing Services, Inc.), national mortgage and financial services (Relocation Financial Services, Inc.), and several others. Keep in mind that all of these additional services were still aimed at the same wholesale corporate market that we knew and had been successful at penetrating.

However, as had occurred twenty-five years previously, we made one big mistake and learned, once again, that switching from a wholesale market (this time) to a retail market was extremely difficult. Keep in mind, RRI was focused exclusively on the wholesale market. That is, we sold to one corporation in order to provide services to hundreds—and many times, thousands—of their employees on an ongoing basis.

In the early nineties we purchased and devoted a considerable amount of resources to a mortgage company in California called, interestingly, Relocation Financial Services—the same name as our mortgage company. Yes, they sold mortgages to relocating employees, but not to their companies. In other words, they were strictly a retail operation. And try as we might, we just couldn't integrate that square peg retail operation into our round hole wholesale mindset/operation and ultimately closed it down.

The outer circle team adds strength to the inner circle team, and where indicated, also provides services directly to clients and transferees .

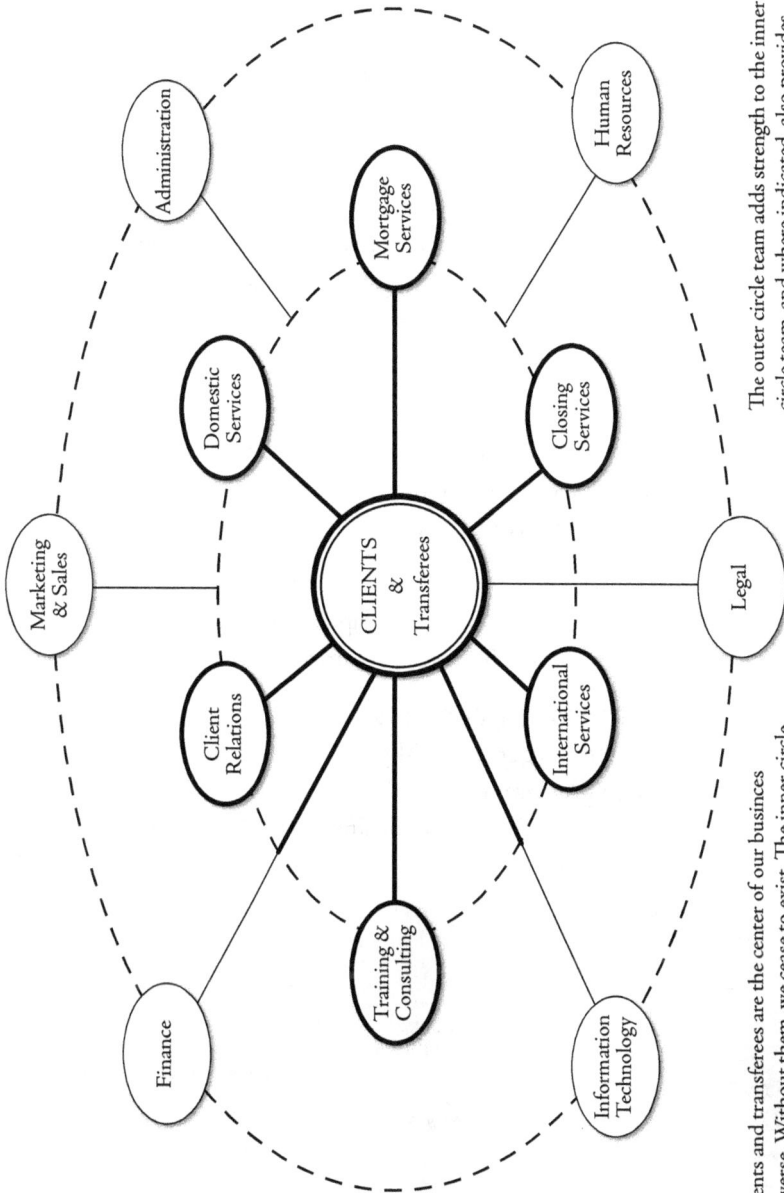

Clients and transferees are the center of our business universe. Without them, we cease to exist. The inner circle team provides services directly to clients and transferees.

PART V HIGHLIGHTS
POINTS TO REMEMBER

FUNCTION VS. PROCESS
Organize around process, not function. In a participatory, collaborative culture, process groups interrelate and together get the work of the organization done.

THE ELLIPTICAL ORGANIZATION
Organize around the center of your business universe. Create an organization without boundaries that's dedicated to doing what has to be done to satisfy customer needs.

CORE PROCESSES/COMPETENCIES
Clearly understand core processes (how you make money). Core competencies must mirror processes. Outsource everything else.

BUSINESS PROCESS OUTSOURCING (BPO)
Attach 70 percent value to capabilities and mutual comfort zone and 30 percent to price.

MIGRATING THE BUSINESS MODEL
Stay within your established "wholesale" or "retail" marketing environment; migrate into new activities carefully only after current business is well established and profitable.

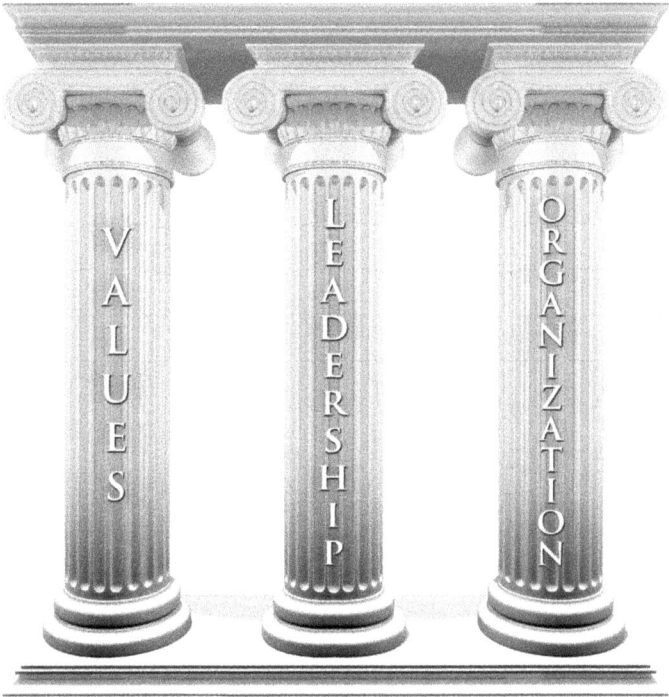

"How Lucky We Are"

In the Introduction I said: "I'm indebted to this great country of ours for providing the environment for entrepreneurs like myself that allows us to grow personally and professionally - to be all we can be."

I always knew I was lucky to be born and brought up in America, but it was not until the nineties, when we started to travel the world, that I came to appreciate just how unbelievably lucky we Americans are.

HOW BUSINESS CAN CHANGE THE WORLD

During a trip to Egypt in the early part of 2001, my wife and I were dismayed to learn that unemployment topped 50 percent, which was manifested in many ways, including an escalating crime rate. Other examples abounded: one of our taxi drivers was a medical doctor by training; another was a lawyer. Our guide, with a master's degree in Egyptology, worked for a pittance-when he could get work-and his fondest hope was to join his sister, a medical doctor in America.

Having been in the Middle East at the time and reflecting on it since that time, fortifies my belief that one of the root causes of activist Arab/Muslim extremism is the fact that their leaders (dictators in many cases) have let them down over the years by suppressing their citizens and avoiding and/or squelching anything that would encourage an expanding business environment. There has been little productive work or wages for their people. Put another way, they are not providing something of value for their people that would keep their energies positively occupied and directed, as apposed to involvement in ideological fanaticism and war. As my grandmother used to say," idleness is the devil's helper."

As I write this, I am so pleased that Turkey's application for EU membership appears to be moving along on a positive track. It will take several economic success stories in the Middle East to make any headway in giving their people a viable alternative to religious fanaticism and war.

WE KNOW HOW LUCKY WE ARE

Not too long ago, my wife and I took a taxi ride from downtown San Francisco to the airport, and as was our habit, we engaged the driver in conversation. He was a Vietnamese who had been in the United States for about ten years, had gradually brought his family over to this country, and had built two successful businesses, one of which was his taxi company. He was proud and happy and thrilled to share his pride and thoughts. Shortly before we arrived at the airport, I asked him to what he attributed his success in his new country. Without hesitation he said, "We know how lucky we are".

My most fervent hope is that the majority of registered voters in these United States really appreciate how lucky we are and how we became a place on this planet where citizens were not restricted by big government making it difficult to be all you are capable of becoming.

However, as I write this in the summer of 2009, I'm beginning to get concerned about the direction in which America is now headed: not just big government (with its attendant big debt, taxes and regulations) - but what appears to be anti-business.

SMALL BUSINESS, ENTREPRENEURS, INNOVATION, JOBS

According to the Small Business Administration, the USA's 27.2 million small businesses are the major engine of our economic growth, and therefore, jobs and prosperity. According to the SBA, they represent 99.7% of all employer firms and 97.3% of all the exporters of goods. Also, the SBA states that they generate the majority of innovations that come from U.S. companies. Innovation comes from entrepreneurs and creates new businesses and jobs - and I believe entrepreneurs have been the single, biggest factor taking us out of past recessions.

When the Obama Administration rushed through its $787,000,000,000 "stimulus" package, small business had no input and received no direct "stimulus". Once I studied the situation it became apparent that this was to be expected because, without exception, the Administration's people with responsibility for the economy came from a lifetime in politics, public service and academia. How can the world of business - let alone small business - be anything but an abstraction to this group?

That's why I'm concerned for the future of small business, entrepreneurs, innovation and new job creation. Therefore, I'm concerned for the future of America and the fact that many voters will realize too late how lucky we used to be. Calvin Coolidge said, "The business of America is business." Free enterprise has always been the core of American culture - and I believe it is now under assault as never before.

YOU CAN DO SOMETHING ABOUT IT

If you feel as strongly as I do about the change in direction coming out of Washington, I encourage you to be aware, get involved and make your feelings known. Communicate repeatedly with your Senators and Representative at both the federal and state level - by telephone, e-mail, snail mail or whatever means available. Seek out like-minded individuals and share your thoughts, Seek out those with opposing views, hear them out respectfully and point out things they may not have been aware of. If enough voters come forward and take a stand for free enterprise we have a reasonable chance that the America of traditional values won't be lost forever.

Acknowledgments

I'm so very fortunate to have a wide circle of intelligent and well-read friends, business acquaintances, and, of course, family. I utilized them all in the development of this book.

They all knew me well enough to know that when I asked them to critique the first draft, I wanted to be told exactly the way they felt about it, versus telling me what most authors want to hear, i.e., "Your book is wonderful and needs no editing."

Well, they told me the way it was (as usual, a humbling experience) and repeated that exercise on the next two drafts. No doubt they added substantially to the content, for which I am most indebted.

First, I need to acknowledge my wife, best friend, and partner, Judy, who was my constant proofreader, critic, and general overall helpmate all the way.

The varsity team that served as the primary critics were Alan Anderson, Sam Baresse, Joe Benevides, Marty and Joan Blaustein, Sean Casey, Dan Champ, Bob Fraser, Jonathan Hall, Tom Janes, Tim McCarney, Sue Rose, Louis "Skip" Schippers, Loren Schulenberg, Ed Washington, and Dick Weisberg.

A more diversified group would be hard to find. They included a commercial banker, a dentist, a teacher, a doctor of psychology, an investment banker, a director of marketing, a human resources expert, the general manager of a radio station, a few high-level executives, and several successful small business owners, to name a few.

A special note of appreciation goes to Karen Troupe, who always bailed me out when I had problems with the word-processing program on my computer.

And a very special thanks to my great right hand of thirty-four years, Nancy Doherty. She is a true executive secretary of the first order. Even in retirement she proved she was still the best proofreader in the business.

I owe all these friends, business acquaintances, and family members a deep debt of gratitude. Thank you, one and all!

Bibliography

Bennis, Warren, and Burt Nanus. *Leaders: The Strategies for Taking Charge.* New York: Harper & Row, 1985.

Bennis, Warren. *On Becoming a Leader.* Reading, MA: Addison-Wesley, 1989.

———. *Why Leaders Can't Lead.* San Francisco: Jossey-Bass, 1989.

———. *An Invented Life: Reflections on Leadership and Change.* Reading, MA: Addison-Wesley, 1993.

Drucker, Peter. *The Practice of Management.* New York: Harper & Row, 1954.

———. *Managing for Results.* London: Heinemann, 1964.

———. *The Effective Executive.* New York: Harper & Row, 1967.

———. *The Age of Discontinuity.* London: Heinemann, 1969.

———. *Managing in Turbulent Times.* New York: Harper & Row, 1980.

———. *Innovation and Entrepreneurship.* London: Heinemann, 1985.

———. *The Frontiers of Management.* London: Heinemann, 1995.

Handy, Charles. *Understanding Organizations.* London: Penguin Books, 1976.

———. *Gods of Management.* London: Business Books, 1978.

———. *The Future of Work.* Oxford: Basil Clackwell, 1984.

———, and J. Constable. *The Making of Managers.* London: Longman, 1988.

———. *The Age of Unreason.* London: Business Books, 1989.

———. *Inside Organizations: 21 Ideas for Managers.* London: BBC Books, 1990.

———. *Beyond Certainty: The Changing World of Organizations.* London: Century, 1995.

Herzberg, Frederick. *The Motivation to Work.* New York: John Wiley, 1959.

Levitt, Ted. *Innovation in Marketing.* New York: McGraw Hill, 1962.

———. *The Marketing Mode.* New York: McGraw Hill, 1969.

———. *The Marketing Imagination.* New York: Free Press, 1983.

———. *Thinking About Management.* New York: Free Press, 1991.

Maslow, Abraham. *Motivation and Personality.* New York: Harper & Row, 1954.

McGregor, Douglas. *The Human Side of Enterprise.* New York: McGraw Hill, 1960.

Ohmae, Kenichi. *The Mind of the Strategist.* New York: McGraw Hill, 1982.

———. *Triad Power: The Coming Shape of Global Competition.* New York: Free Press, 1985.

———. *The Borderless World.* London: William Collins, 1990.

Peters, Tom, and Robert Waterman. *In Search of Excellence.* New York and London: Harper & Row, 1982.

Peters, Tom, and Nancy Austin. *A Passion for Excellence.* London: Collins, 1985.

Senge, Peter. *The Fifth Discipline: The Art and Practice of the Learning Organization.* New York: Doubleday, 1990.

Treacy, Michael, and Fred Wiersema. *The Discipline of Market Leaders.* Reading, MA: Addison-Wesley, 1994.

Watson, Thomas Jr. *A Business and Its Beliefs: The Ideas that Helped Build IBM.* New York: McGraw Hill, 1963.

Index

Auctoris
Press

www.auctorispresspub.com
www.talentsolution.net